S Hackett

WJEC EDUQAS GCSE English Language
Teacher's Book

Paula Adair
Jane Sheldon
Jamie Rees

Series Editors:
Jonathan Harrington
Paula Adair

DL DYNAMIC LEARNING

HODDER EDUCATION
AN HACHETTE UK COMPANY

The publisher would like to thank the following for permission to reproduce copyright material:

Acknowledgments:

WJEC Eduqas Assessment Objectives throughout; **p.2** from 'Winter Sports around the UK' from *The Guardian* (The Guardian, 11th January 2014), copyright Guardian News & Media Ltd 2014, reproduced by permission of the publisher; **pp.4–5** Louis Emanuel: from 'Bristol adventurer Lewis Clarke back to being just another student' from *The Bristol Post* (The Bristol Post, 28th January 2014); **p.7** Charlotte Bronte: from a letter to Ellen (October 29th, 1848); **p.9** Alexander McCall Smith: from *44 Scotland Street* (Abacus, 2005); **p.13** from 'The Prize Pugs of America and England' (1891); **p.13** from "Handbag' dogs- Why you should never see your pet as a fashion accessory' (Pets4Homes, 2014), www.Pets4Homes.co.uk; **p.22** Juliette Garside: from 'Ofcom: six-year-olds understand digital technology better than adults' from *The Guardian* (The Guardian, 7th August 2014), copyright Guardian News & Media Ltd 2014, reproduced by permission of the publisher; **pp.30–31**, **45–46** Alexander McCall Smith: from *Tears Of The Giraffe (No. 1 Ladies' Detective Agency)* (Abacus, 2003); **pp.36–37** Adam Edwards: from 'The rise and fall of Mr Fox' from *The Telegraph* (The Telegraph, 5th November 2010), reproduced by permission of Telegraph Media Group; **pp.37–38** John Humphrys: from "WASTE NOT, WANT NOT" – The Proverb We All Forgot' from *The Sunday Times* (The Sunday Times, 9th April 2000); **pp.67–68** Mark Twain: from *The Innocents Abroad* (1869); **p.74** Lizzie Porter: from 'How Wales got cool' from *The Telegraph* (The Telegraph, 9th July 2014), reproduced by permission of Telegraph Media Group; **p.76** from 'How green are our Valleys? ... VERY!' from *The Valleys of South Wales* (Visit Wales, 2015), www.visitwales.com; **p.76** Gareth Johnson: from 'Gay kings, coal miners, whisky, waterfalls and bike riding in the valleys of South Wales' from *Gay Star News* (GSN, 17th February 2013), reproduced by permission of the publisher; **pp.77–78** Helen Pidd: from 'Village shares its Billy Elliot stories at live screening of West End show' from *The Guardian* (The Guardian, 28th September 2014), copyright Guardian News & Media Ltd 2014, reproduced by permission of the publisher.

Every effort has been made to trace or contact all copyright holders, but if any have been inadvertently overlooked the Publishers will be pleased to make the necessary arrangements at the first opportunity.

Although every effort has been made to ensure that website addresses are correct at time of going to press, Hodder Education cannot be held responsible for the content of any website mentioned. It is sometimes possible to find a relocated web page by typing in the address of the home page for a website in the URL window of your browser.

Orders: please contact Bookpoint Ltd, 130 Milton Park, Abingdon, Oxon OX14 4SB. Telephone: (44) 01235 827720. Fax: (44) 01235 400454. Lines are open 9.00–17.00, Monday to Saturday, with a 24-hour message answering service. Visit our website at www.hoddereducation.co.uk

© Paula Adair 2015

First published in 2015 by

Hodder Education

An Hachette UK Company,

338 Euston Road

London NW1 3BH

Impression number	5	4	3	2	1
Year	2019	2018	2017	2016	2015

All rights reserved. Apart from any use permitted under UK copyright law, no part of this publication may be reproduced or transmitted in any form or by any means, electronic or mechanical, including photocopying and recording, or held within any information storage and retrieval system, without permission in writing from the publisher or under licence from the Copyright Licensing Agency Limited. Further details of such licences (for reprographic reproduction) may be obtained from the Copyright Licensing Agency Limited, Saffron House, 6–10 Kirby Street, London EC1N 8TS.

Cover photo (and repeated use throughout) by Ria Osborne

Typeset in 11/14 pt Chaparral Pro Light by Integra Software Services Pvt. Ltd., Pondicherry, India

Printed in the UK by Hobbs the Printers Ltd.

A catalogue record for this title is available from the British Library

ISBN 9781471831874

Contents

Series editor introduction — v

Reading Units

Unit 1	Extracting key information	1
Unit 2	Interpreting information	6
Unit 3	Synthesising information	11
Unit 4	Types of information	19
Unit 5	Explaining language	26
Unit 6	Talking about language	32
Unit 7	Analysing language	40
Unit 8	Comparing writers' ideas	49
Unit 9	Comparing language	57
Unit 10	Using textual references	63
Unit 11	Evaluating critically	70

Writing Units

Unit 12	Communicating clearly and effectively	80
Unit 13	Communicating imaginatively	89
Unit 14	Style and register, purpose and audience	97
Unit 15	Transactional and persuasive writing	107

Introduction

This Teacher's Book gives you the chance to build a programme for students to develop all the skills they will need for the new WJEC Eduqas GCSE in English Language. For the new GCSE there are two exams, called Component One and Component Two.

The exams

- **Component One** is also called 20th Century Literature Reading and Creative Prose Writing. For this students will need to answer questions about an extract (of about 60–100 lines) of literature from the 20th century and also complete a creative writing task from a selection of four titles. This exam lasts for one hour and 45 minutes.

- **Component Two** is also called 19th and 21st Century Non-Fiction Reading and Transactional/Persuasive Writing. In this exam students will need to answer questions about two extracts, totalling about 900–1200 words, of high quality non-fiction writing from the 19th and 21st centuries. They will also need to complete two transactional/persuasive writing tasks. This exam lasts for two hours.

The Student's Book takes them through every one of the skills that are being assessed in this GCSE and shows students how to improve and become more confident in using these skills so that they can do as well as possible in the exams. The structure of this teacher's book helps you to plan this learning over the GCSE course, developing each strand of each Assessment Outcome in three clear stages so that you can be confident that students are exam ready.

Alongside Dynamic Learning Resources this book supports and expands this programme of learning to provide full preparation for the Eduqas GCSE in English Language.

Please remember

None of the activities in this book are actual exam questions but they all focus on the skills assessed in the two components of the WJEC Eduqas English Language exams. None of the approaches suggested in this book, such as Point, Evidence, Explanation are recommended by Eduqas as the only way of setting about particular tasks but are offered here as various ways to help students meet the demands of the examinations.

As well as learning how to complete the various tasks in the exams students will also be encouraged to mark their own work and sample answers so that they can see what is needed for success. The Marking grids used for the activities are not meant to represent the full sets of marking criteria available in the Sample Assessment Materials from Eduqas but are there to give students the chance to assess their own work against the skills required under each AO.

Unit 1
Extracting key information

LEARNING OBJECTIVES

▶ To recognise questions asking for specific information
▶ To work systematically through a text, selecting relevant information
▶ To present the extracted information appropriately

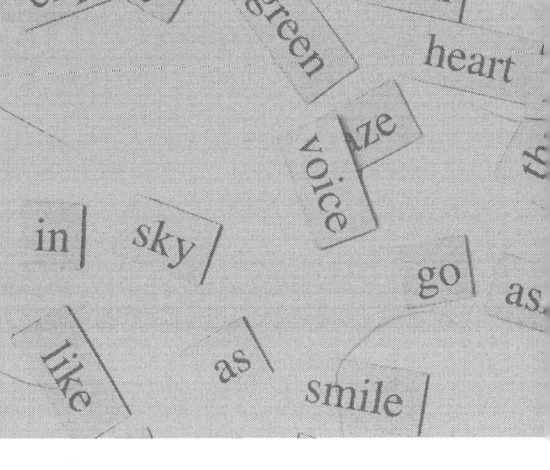

Assessment Objectives

AO1 ■ Identify and interpret explicit information and ideas

Get going

Step 1 | Work on your skills

Depending on the age and ability of your students, you may want to spend a short time discussing some of the strategies for looking at unseen texts.

Get students to come up with their own definitions of the following terms. Display agreed class definitions for future reference.

- Purpose – for example, what a text is for. Generally, to entertain, persuade or inform. Often, a combination of two or more of these.
- Layout – for example, this will often give clues as to what a text is about. For example, a chart, table or bullet points will suggest an informative text.
- Audience – for example, who the text is aimed at. This will affect the style and features of the writing.

A general understanding of these features is key to discussion of any text. You may want to explore this in some more detail.

Starter activity

If you have students who find the unseen texts a little daunting, it may be useful to provide them with some strategies and approaches to reading unfamiliar texts. The following information can be used in lots of ways – as a class discussion, as a modelled, reading activity by the teacher or, as here, as a thinking skills, ranking activity.

Number each technique in terms of usefulness when reading a new text. Use a 1–10 scale. 1 = Not at all useful. 10 = Fantastic! A 'must use'. (Tip: Avoid the number 7.)

Reading technique	How useful is this technique?
Use the heading – think about what it is saying. Make a prediction about the topic and the viewpoint of the writer.	
Think about what you already know about the topic.	
Use information such as photos, diagrams or charts to aid your understanding.	
Use any information given on the exam paper about a text to help your initial understanding.	
Use the punctuation to aid your understanding – read complete sentences (stop at full stops) and remember why we use commas.	
At the end of every paragraph, pause and review what you have just read. Has it gone into your head or did your mind wander? Sum it up and think of questions that may have formed in your mind about the text.	

Reading Units

Reading technique		How useful is this technique?
Use a ruler or other device to focus on sentences or paragraphs in sequence. This stops you skipping important information.		
Use strategies to tackle unfamiliar words.	Read in context (what came before the word and what comes after) and have an 'educated guess' at what it might mean.	
	Look to see if any part of the word reminds you of another related word that you may know the meaning of already.	
	If all fails, read the sentence without the word – often you can understand the wider meaning without it.	
This may sound strange, but the exam texts are often about interesting, engaging subjects. Visualise in your head what you are reading and enjoy what you are reading.		

ACTIVITY 1

These techniques can be immediately practised on the 'Winter sports around the UK' text.

This activity can also be used by students to provide practice in highlighting key words in the questions and scanning/highlighting quickly in the text.

This would be a good exercise to turn into a timed competition (girls against boys; or gold, silver and bronze awards).

Extension Activity

Provide students with this extra text to read and then ask them to answer the questions that follow.

Snow walking

Snowfall in the UK is rarely heavy enough, but if there's a deep drift, snap some snowshoes over regular walking shoes, and go for it. Remember though – safety first. Use poles, avoid groomed ski courses and be aware of what to do in event of avalanches.

Snow tubing

'Tubing' is riding a doughnut-shaped inflatable tube around a specially designed course. It's a comfier ride than tobogganing, and even more exhilarating. For the thrill-seeking but ice-phobic, the Viper slide at Chatham Ski Slope is an 80-metre dry course.

Nordic skiing

More varied (and harder!) than the Alpine variety, Nordic skiing is similar to cross-country skiing, but with ski jumps. Participants are attached to their skis at the toe only, so they can push forwards or go uphill. Nordic skiing was even the first ski event to feature in a Winter Olympics.

Ice climbing

Hack your way up 15 metres of ice at the largest indoor ice wall in the world at Ice Factor in Kinlochleven. There are courses for all levels of experience; taster sessions are £30 an adult including equipment hire and instructor.

a Identify three pieces of safety advice given to snow walkers. [3]
b What was the first ski event to feature in the Winter Olympics? [1]
c How high is the largest indoor ice wall in the world? [1]

Answers

a Any three of the following:
- Use snowshoes over regular walking shoes.
- Use poles.
- Avoid groomed ski courses.
- Be aware of what to do in event of avalanches. [3]

b Nordic skiing [1]
c 15 metres [1]

Unit 1 Extracting key information

Students should be directed to do the following:

- Remember the number of marks reflects the number of answers.
- Be selective – answer the question by precisely picking out the information needed.
- Don't waste time by using long sentences if they are not needed.
- Use scanning and highlighting techniques to work quickly and effectively through the questions.

Step 2 Practise your skills

ACTIVITY 2

When scanning, students could use these methods to speed things up:

- Scan for the key word from a question.
- Predict what you are looking for – for example, is it a name or a number?
- If you are looking for a name or a place, look for a capital letter.
- Use the features (for example, headings) to focus your scanning.

ACTIVITY 3

Suggested questions to the Lewis Clarke activity:

a Where did Lewis begin his journey? [1]
b What date did Lewis start his journey? [1]
c How many miles did Lewis cover? [1]
d What was the date of arrival at the South Pole? [1]
e How many re-supplies did Lewis receive? [1]
f Which day did Lewis have off? [1]
g How old is Lewis? [1]
h How low could the temperature drop? [1]

Step 3 Challenge yourself

ACTIVITY 4

You could differentiate this activity by adding extra elements to the question, such as grouping the problems into the environment and then physical/psychological effects.

For example:

List five of the environmental problems the men faced on their expedition. [5]

or

List five of the physical/psychological problems the men faced on their expedition. [5]

Award one mark for each correct answer.

Environmental

- crevasses/huge cracks in ice, hidden by snow
- had to cover 481 miles
- bitterly cold winds
- very low temperatures/–50°C
- white-outs
- hostile terrain

Physical/psychological

- thought they were going to die
- started to panic
- tougher than expected/'a toll on our bodies'/'hardest thing'
- frostbite (on nose and on fingers)
- burnt lips
- blisters
- hypothermia
- thought they'd not finish
- pneumonia
- chest infections
- every day was gruelling (16 hours a day skiing/only four hours sleep a day)

ACTIVITY 5

If the answers are written in a paragraph, students should underline the individual points (up to 5 marks).

BE EXAM READY

LEARNING OBJECTIVES

▶ To practice answering a question
▶ To mark my own response using a mark scheme
▶ To assess sample answers to the exam question

Question 1

Students have to respond to this question:

List ten events in which British competitors won gold medals in the London Olympics, according to the newspaper article. [10]

Answer A – 0 marks

Feedback: Wrong answers – hasn't focused on the key words in the question (British and events)

Answer B – 3 marks

Feedback: Three good answers, but should be written in the order they appear (tracking)

Not precise enough with cycling and sprinting

Answer C – 10 marks

Feedback: Full marks. Precise and ordered. 11 answers given, only 10 needed but one extra to 'make sure' is not a bad thing!

Extension Activity

Spend 10 minutes reading the Bristol Post article about Lewis Clarke and answering the question that follows:

Bristol adventurer Lewis Clarke back to being just another student

RECORD-breaking teenager Lewis Clarke returned to the seat in his chemistry class which has been empty for almost two months.

The recently-crowned youngest person to ski to the South Pole had his head buried in the books as he knuckled down for his GCSEs this summer.

Lewis, 16, trekked 702 miles across over one of the most inhospitable landscapes on earth where he faced 49 punishing days with temperatures as low as -50°C and winds of up to 120mph.

Arriving at Queen Elizabeth's Hospital School yesterday morning, the intrepid adventurer said he had had little time to adjust to life back home following his return last Friday.

'It still feels very weird. I have been slipping back into it slowly but it feels strange to come here and see all my friends just getting on with their schoolwork.

'It was something almost impossible to imagine when I was out there facing the antarctic winds day after day.'

Lewis spent the weekend in TV and radio studios giving interviews and recounting his journey. He has also given talks on his adventure, sharing the stage with Sir Ranulph Fiennes on one occasion.

He said: 'It has been very surreal. As soon as I was back there were cameras and interviews and I have been calling in to radio stations and appearing on television. It's been non-stop.

'It was such a quick change from being out in the wilderness spending every day with one guy and lugging my stuff across the snow. It is bizarre to think how normal life here has just continued.'

Recounting the moment the South Pole came into sight for the first time at around 2pm on the final day of his challenge, he said: 'It was amazing, having been going towards this goal

Unit 1 Extracting key information

> the whole time. Sometimes it seemed so far away and getting to see it become a reality was just a relief.'
>
> Lewis is no stranger to a challenge. In September 2012 he and five other 12-year-old swimmers broke the record for the youngest team ever to swim the English Channel.
>
> The crossing took the team 13 and a half hours, during which time the young swimmers had to watch out for jellyfish, passing ships and floating debris.
>
> But, he said the swim paled into insignificance when compared to his latest achievement.
>
> He said: 'It was the hardest thing I have ever done and the hardest thing I ever will do. I can't see anything as difficult as that.'
>
> He said he had no plans what to do next but added that over the summer - after his exams are over - he would give it some thought.
>
> He said: 'I have only just finished this and now I have got to get on with my GCSEs, which should be fine, I hope.'

According to the article, list five of Lewis Clarke's thoughts and feelings now that he has returned home from the South Pole. [5]

Possible answers

- Has had 'little time to adjust to life back home'.
- Feeling very weird/strange to see all his friends 'getting on with their schoolwork'.
- Was 'impossible to imagine' in the Antartic.
- It has been 'surreal' giving TV and radio interviews.
- A 'change' from life in South Pole.
- Feels he won't do anything as hard again.
- No plans about what to do next.

5

Unit 2
Interpreting information

LEARNING OBJECTIVES

▶ To gain an understanding of what it means to 'interpret' information
▶ To be able to recognise questions that ask you to interpret information
▶ To practise working systematically through a text, selecting relevant information and applying an interpretation in order to answer the question

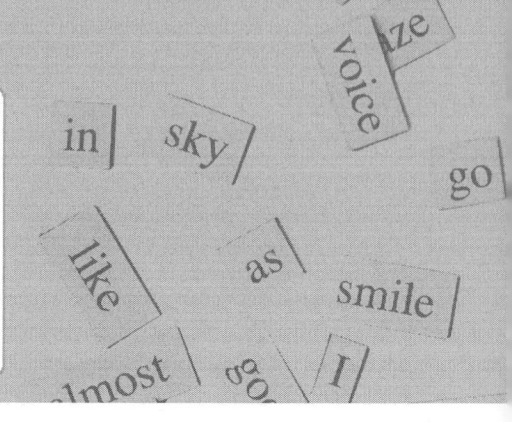

Assessment Objectives

AO1 ▪ Identify and interpret explicit and implicit information and ideas

Get going

Step 1 Work on your skills

ACTIVITY 1

Possible answers to the 'interpreting phrases' activity:

- Add insult to injury – Make a bad situation worse
- A blessing in disguise – Something that seems bad at first may turn out to be good
- Read between the lines – Work out something that is hinted at
- Add fuel to the fire – Make a bad situation worse (normally an argument or angry situation)
- Feather your own nest – Make yourself rich (perhaps dishonestly)

Discussion could take place around the idea that 'Add insult to injury' and 'Add fuel to the fire' mean similar things. Students could look for similar idioms around the other phrases.

In the reverse activity, the following definitions could be used as prompts:

- People and things are not always what they seem – Don't judge a book by its cover
- There is a something obvious not being spoken about – The elephant in the room

- Talking alone does not make things happen – Fine words butter no parsnips
- Looking in the wrong place or accusing the wrong person – Barking up the wrong tree
- To deliberately present a counter argument in order to get a reaction – Play Devil's advocate

This could be played as a game in class – read the definition and guess the correct answer. A good homework activity is to find ten more phrases.

ACTIVITY 2

Students' completed tables may look like this. The answers given here could be useful for peer- or self-assessment.

Evidence	Interpretation
'resentment of success'	Hates that it makes so much money and is so popular
'like the Wild West'	Rough, dangerous and busy
'like a plague of locusts, stealing tents and their contents'	No care taken. Destroying anything in their path
'delays'	Very congested – akin to airports
'people who go there'	He dislikes the people who go there rather than the organisers.

Unit 2 Interpreting information

Evidence	Interpretation
'there just so they can talk about it afterwards'	People only going to 'say they have been' – they don't really enjoy it.
'we can barely hear the band, let alone see them'	It's not a good physical experience – sound and sight quality is poor.
'all those flags'	The national pride gets on his nerves.
'incessant milling around'	Nothing to do but wander.
'you have to pay over the odds'	It's expensive – more money than it's worth.
'a watery pint of beer in a flimsy plastic glass'	The quality of beer is poor.
'the cost of a week's holiday'	It costs a lot – could be spent elsewhere.
'war zone'	It's not relaxing – you don't feel rested.

ACTIVITY 3

The following are possible responses to what it means to interpret information.

- To explaining the meaning behind something.
- To discuss the meaning of something that is not immediately obvious.
- To present the information in a different way.
- To give your own thoughts on words or phrases.

These could be offered up as starting points for the students' own definition. Another activity is to combine all these responses into one definition.

Step 2 Practise your skills

ACTIVITY 4

Below are quotations from the Charlotte Brontë letter. Students could use these to match to the interpretations on page 13 of the Student's Book.

'my life is not so varied that … much should have occurred worthy of mention.'	'The late sad event has, I feel, made me more apprehensive'
'I have now nearly got over the effects of my late illness'	'I cannot help feeling much depressed sometimes.'

'I feel much more uneasy about my sisters than myself just now.'	'faith and resignation are difficult to practise under some circumstances.'
'It is useless to question her – you get no answers.'	'The weather has been most unfavourable'
'I could not, and would not, leave home on any account.'	'They must leave us, or we must leave them, one day.'

Again, the answers given here could prove useful for peer- or self-assessment.

Interpretation	Evidence in letter
Nothing much has happened to her in the past week.	'my life is not so varied that … much should have occurred worthy of mention.'
She has not been well lately.	'I have now nearly got over the effects of my late illness'
She is worried about her sisters, especially Emily's appearance and physical health.	'I feel much more uneasy about my sisters than myself just now.'
Her sister will not speak about her illness or take advice/medicine.	'It is useless to question her – you get no answers.'
The death of her brother has unsettled her.	'The late sad event has, I feel, made me more apprehensive'
She feels depressed.	'I cannot help feeling much depressed sometimes.'
Her faith in God is being tested.	'faith and resignation are difficult to practise under some circumstances.'
The weather has been bad.	'The weather has been most unfavourable'
She is unable/unwilling to leave home.	'I could not, and would not, leave home on any account.'
She is too aware of how brief life can be.	'They must leave us, or we must leave them, one day.'

Reading Units

Step 3 | Challenge yourself

ACTIVITY 5

Ensure that students differentiate between the two bullet points in this activity. Consider which points in the mark scheme address the first bullet point (facts and details about Justo) and which address the second (the kind of person he is). Students could do this with two coloured highlighting pens.

Mark scheme

0 marks	Nothing worthy of credit.
1 mark	One or two unsupported points or simple comments with very brief, occasional reference to the text, or copy unselectively.
2–4 marks	Simple comments based on surface features of the text. Limited in inference.
5–7 marks	Appropriate detail from the text selected to show understanding of the character. These answers should be making valid inferences.
8–10 marks	Appropriate detail from the text explored with depth and insight. These answers should be thorough as well as perceptive, covering a range of points accurately and with an assured grasp of character. Inferences should be thoughtful and assured.

Below are some points showing evidence of students' understanding:

- His 'reputation' has spread to other villages.
- People say he is 'a defender of causes' (he can stick up for himself, or others).
- He is also 'a wit'.
- He is perhaps 'too eager' to create his own 'mythology'.
- He is 'one to watch' in the strength events.
- He is clearly very strong (whether or not the ox story is true).
- He jokes about the 'ox story'.
- He is the largest man in the competition.
- He goes barefoot in the wood chopping because he only has one pair of boots.
- He has lost a toe.
- He can't afford new boots.
- He is much better than anyone else at the wood-chopping.
- He is less impressive at wine drinking.
- He is formidably strong in the 'farmer's walk'.
- He plays out a 'false drama' for the crowd.
- He acknowledges his admirers.
- He jokes with the children.

Overview:

- He is well known.
- He is immensely strong.
- He has a sense of humour/is a practical joker.
- He is humble/modest (false?).
- He is perhaps rather proud of himself/likes to be the centre of attention.
- He is a bit of a 'show-off'.
- He is not wealthy.
- He is fearless.
- He relates well to people.

BE EXAM READY

LEARNING OBJECTIVES

▶ To put into practice everything learnt so far on interpreting information
▶ To practise these skills under timed pressure

Question 1
Possible answers

- He won't now give his real name in case he's targeted by animal rights activists.
- Dave now has regular cases of TB in his herd.
- A member of his own family 'came down' with TB.
- He now has badgers on his land.
- In 1998, fewer than 6,000 cows killed because of TB; in 2011, figure rose to 34,000.
- TB in cows has 'increased dramatically' since 1992/was under control in 1970s/1980s.
- TB in cattle has resulted in a decrease in the number of dairy farms.
- Farmers are now not allowed to shoot badgers/badgers are now protected.
- Their numbers have got out of control/numbers have 'grown considerably'.
- Badgers have no natural predators.
- Farmers work very long hours every day of the week.
- Its 'hands-on'/intensive work – nursing them through birth/hand feeding when sick.
- Some farmers have gone out of business – 40% of dairy farms have stopped farming.
- The money they receive from milk has been 'slashed'.
- Bad weather can make things worse for farmers.
- The price of grain has increased and has hit farmers hard.

Extension Activity

Give students the following question and extract to consolidate their learning in this unit.

You have 10 minutes to read the following and answer the question that follows it:

> **This extract is about a young boy called Bertie who lives in Edinburgh. Irene is his mother.**
>
> 'Hurry up now, Bertie,' said Irene. 'It's almost ten o'clock, and if we don't get there in time you may not get your audition. Now, you wouldn't want that, would you?'
>
> Bertie sighed. To miss the audition was exactly what he would want, but he realised that it was fruitless to protest. Once his mother had seen a notice about the Edinburgh Teenage Orchestra, she had immediately put his name down for an audition.
>
> 'Do you realise how exciting this is?' she said to Bertie. 'This orchestra is planning to do a concert in Paris in a couple of weeks. Wouldn't you just love that?'
>
> Bertie frowned. The name of the orchestra suggested that it was for teenagers and he was barely six. 'Couldn't I just audition in seven years' time?' he asked his mother. 'I'll be a teenager then.'
>
> 'If you're worried about being the youngest one there,' said Irene reassuringly, 'then you shouldn't! The fact that it's called the Edinburgh Teenage Orchestra is neither here nor there. The word teenage is just to indicate what standard is required.'
>
> 'But I'm not a teenager,' protested Bertie helplessly. 'They'll all be teenagers. I promise you. I'll be the only one in dungarees.'
>
> 'There may well be others in dungarees,' said Irene. 'And anyway, once you're sitting down behind your music stand, nobody will notice what you're wearing.'

9

Reading Units

What are your impressions of Bertie and Irene and the relationship between them in these lines? [10]

You must refer to the text to support your answer.

Possible answers

- Irene is sure that Bertie wants an audition and wouldn't want to miss out.
- Bertie 'sighs', revealing his lack of enthusiasm and that this is only too familiar.
- He knows it is 'fruitless to protest'.
- She had put his name down 'immediately'.
- She is convinced that Bertie will 'love' the Paris trip.
- Bertie 'frowns' and tries to point out that he is not yet a teenager.
- Irene speaks 'reassuringly' and dismisses his point about his age.
- Bertie protests but 'helplessly'.
- He says he will be the only one in dungarees, trying to reason with her.
- Irene brushes that aside.

Overview:

- She has faith in him.
- She is a 'pushy' parent/full of maternal pride.
- She doesn't listen to him/is self-absorbed/oblivious to his feelings/selfish.
- She imposes her enthusiasms on him/lives her dreams through him.
- She is in control/bossy/impossible/persistent.
- He is mature for his years (more mature than Irene!)/intelligent.
- He knows her better than she knows him/she misunderstands him.
- He is the victim of her ambition/knows he will be humiliated.
- She is determined/what 'she' wants is what 'he' wants.
- He seems resigned but resists (reluctant).

Mark scheme

0 marks	Nothing worthy of credit
1 mark	One or two unsupported points or simple comments; very brief, occasional reference to the text; copying unselectively.
2–4 marks	Simple comments based on surface features of the text. Limited in inference.
5–7 marks	Appropriate detail from the text selected to show understanding of the characters. These answers should be making valid interpretations.
8–10 marks	Appropriate detail from the text explored with depth and insight. These answers should be thorough as well as perceptive, covering a range of points accurately and with an assured grasp of character. Inferences should be thoughtful and assured.

Unit 3
Synthesising information

LEARNING OBJECTIVES

▶ To understand what is meant by synthesising information
▶ To select information from different parts of a text or texts
▶ To combine different pieces of information in your answer

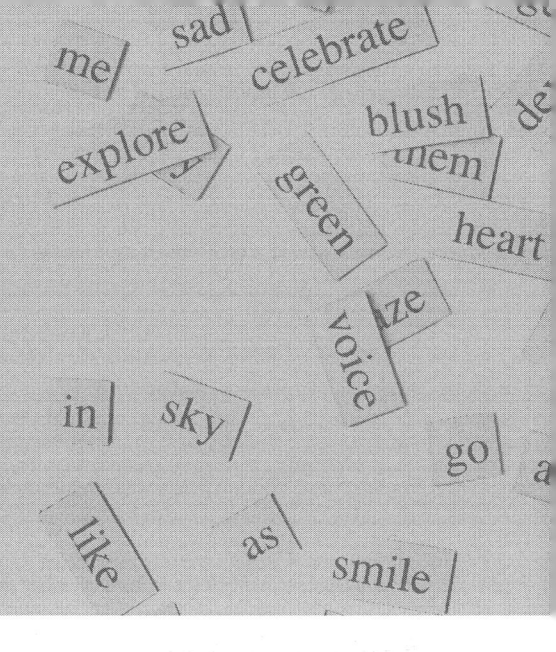

This unit helps to prepare students for Section A of Component 2 of the written examination: 19th and 21st century non-fiction reading. The time allocation for this section is 1 hour, comprising 10 minutes' reading and 50 minutes' writing. It is worth 40 marks – 30% of the qualification.

Candidates are assessed on their understanding of two extracts (about 900–1200 words in total) of high-quality non-fiction writing, one from the 19th century, the other from the 21st century, assessed through a range of structured questions. This section assesses AO1, AO2, AO3 and AO4. The following unit deals with assessment objectives AO1 and AO3.

Assessment Objectives

AO1 ■ Identify and interpret explicit and implicit information and ideas.
AO3 ■ Compare writers' ideas and perspectives, as well as how these are conveyed, across two or more texts.

To begin

Begin by asking students:

- What does synthesis mean?

A definition is given in the Student's Book but you may want students to use a dictionary to come up with a more detailed definition. They may also be able to define what synthesis means in science lessons, which may help them to understand the term further.

Students should understand the purpose of the tasks that follow. The Eduqas specification states that candidates should be able to:

- identify and interpret ideas and information in a range of literature
- select and summarise ideas and information from a single text, synthesising from more than one text
- evaluate a writer's choice of vocabulary, grammatical and structural features
- compare texts critically with respect to the above.

The unit activities address these requirements. The Student's Book identifies four steps by which this will be done.

1 Identify the demands of the question.
2 Locate the information you need in the first text.
3 Locate the information you need in the second text.
4 Combine this information to form your answer.

Get going

Step 1 Work on your skills

ACTIVITY 1

Here, students practise identifying the demands of the question.

Students discuss with a learning partner what each instruction in the given table would be asking them to do in the exam. You may wish to provide dictionaries for a less able class.

11

Reading Units

For a more challenging task, students could complete the task without using the word itself. This encourages more searching definitions.

Answers

Term	What it's asking you to do
Find	Locate information
List	Make a record of information, usually ordered with a few words on each line
Explain	Make something clear by giving information about it
Examine	Consider something carefully in order to discover something about it
Explore	Search for and discover something
Compare	Consider similarities
Contrast	Consider differences

As an extension, you could ask students to explain what more difficult terms are asking them to do. They could consider:

- analyse (study in detail)
- discuss (talk or write about a subject in detail, considering different ideas)
- assess (to judge the importance of something).

Draw students' attention to the Top tips:

- 'Explain', 'examine' and 'explore' are not asking students to do widely different things. There is no need to struggle to come up with completely different definitions.
- Explain that the words in the table are imperatives.

Extension Activity

Ask students what the difference is between a **what** question and a **how** question.

- A **what** question is usually a 'search and find' task.
- A **how** question requires analysis of the writer's techniques.

Examples of **what** questions:

a What does the writer mean by 'Time is money' in line 2? [1]
b What does the writer suggest family members should do to help in the house? [2]

Types of synthesis questions

Draw attention to the fact that **what** questions often come earlier in the examination. Considering the allocation of marks is also an indication of the difficulty level of a question and how much information is required.

Some questions have two parts, a **what** and a **how** section.

For example:

c **What** do you think and feel about Lydia M. Child's views about running a household? [10]

You should comment on:

- **what** is said
- **how** it is said.

You must refer to the text to support your comments.

d **How** does John Humphrys try to persuade you that Americans should change their attitude towards food? [10]

You should comment on:

- Humphrys' attitude to waste
- how he gets across his argument.

Following this activity, it is worth distributing past papers to students so that they can familiarise themselves with the wording of a variety of questions.

Students could note down five different questions in their workbooks. These could then be read to a work partner or to the class. Students should then suggest what they would be required to do in response to a particular question type.

Examples of what students might come up with are given below.

a What does the writer mean by 'Time is money' in line 2? [1]

Answer: I would be required to find the expression 'Time is money' in line 2 and for 1 mark, explain briefly **what** the writer means by this.

d **How** does John Humphrys try to persuade you that Americans should change their attitude towards food? [10]

Answer: I would need to use the P-E-E technique and look at a range of the techniques that Humphrys uses in order to persuade the reader that Americans should change their attitude towards food. It is worth 10 marks, so I would need a good range of points.

A progressive difficulty level has been suggested in the questions above.

This is to lead students towards the synthesis question, which is often the last one because it draws on all the skills the students have displayed in the exam so far – **searching**, **finding** and **explaining** – and now asks students to do this across two texts.

Unit 3 Synthesising information

Note that students are often concerned that a compare and contrast question will require them to repeat points that they have made in their earlier responses. They worry that they will be penalised for this. It is worth explaining that they can use these points because now they are using them for a different reason – to cross-reference.

ACTIVITY 2

Answers

A suggested order is: list, find, explain, examine, compare how the writers... but this need not be definitive.

The tasks in earlier activities should help students to explain how they came to their rank order decision.

Step 2 Practise your skills

ACTIVITY 3

Students will need copies of the two text extracts below so that they can add highlighting and underlining.

All possible answers here are underlined.

'Handbag' dogs – Why you should never see your pet as a fashion accessory

Tiny Chihuahuas, teacup Yorkies, Pomeranians and more... The popularity of toy dogs has been on the rise for some years now, leading to a modern phenomenon known as the 'handbag' dog – literally, a toy dog small enough to be carried in an oversized handbag.

This trend for 'handbag' dogs may have begun with celebrity dog lovers such as Paris Hilton and Nicole Richie, but it didn't take long to filter down into the land of us mere mortals too. The image of someone carrying a small dog about in a handbag while they go about their business, something that would once have raised eyebrows, has become incredibly mainstream over the last few years, even within the UK.

Having a toy dog that is the height of fashion and can be carried in a suitably trendy underarm carrier should always be a secondary consideration to actively wanting to own a dog and committing to caring for it for the duration of its life. If you are considering getting a toy dog just because you think they are fashionable or 'cool' or can be ported around in your bag – think again! While undeniably small and cute, toy dogs are still dogs. They require a significant commitment of both time and money to their care and wellbeing, and live for well over a decade in most cases. If you see owning a toy dog a short-term option, something to be discarded when fashions change – walk away now. Battersea Dogs' Home has reported an increase of over 40% during 2012 in the number of toy dogs coming into the shelter for rehoming, with Chihuahuas and Yorkshire Terriers topping the list. Owning a dog of any size is a lifetime commitment. Don't be tempted to buy a toy dog for yourself or your child on a whim.

The Prize Pugs of America and England (1891)

The question is often asked in a critical manner, of what utility is the pug? It has lately become the fashion for some people to buy a pug as they would a diamond pin, a silk hat or fine clothes. Yet, the pug is not just a 'fancy' dog but a good, intelligent watch dog, ever on the alert for an intruder. It is a faithful companion, affectionate in disposition, and, having a fine smooth coat, is easily kept clean in the house. With a little attention given to its teeth, its breath is as free from odour as that of any other dog. Pugs are easily trained, and are, as a rule, good with children, though they should not have to endure having the curl taken out of their tail by a teasing two-year-old. It has been said that pugs are stupid, but such is not the case, and, like any other dog, their intelligence depends upon the attention given them by intelligent people. Bring them up among ignorant, careless people or keep them away from the family, and it follows that they will not display that intelligence which is seen in dogs that are properly trained. Of course to the sportsman or farmer, a pug would be useless, but as a family pet, he is all that can be desired.

Reading Units

You could now ask students what type of questions they are:

- search and find or
- analytical.

Hopefully, they will identify that, even though the questions are phrased 'Give three breeds…' 'Give two reasons…' 'Why is…?' these are still **what** questions that require them simply to locate information.

Step 3 Challenge yourself

ACTIVITY 4

Information that could be considered is underlined in the texts on page 13.

- This question requires search and find skills but also inference.
- Students may also note that some of the information they used to answer the initial questions can be used again.
- Care is needed to ensure that the whole question is answered. Students sometimes **find** relevant information but do not take the next step, which is to ensure that it is embedded in their answer.
- For example, a student writing:

  If you buy a small dog, a 'two-year-old' might like playing with its tail.

  is part of the way to answering the question but has used the information in such a way that they have made it sound as if this is actually a good reason to buy a dog.

Improve your skills

LEARNING OBJECTIVES

▶ To recognise questions that require students to synthesise information
▶ To find the information needed to answer the question
▶ To group this information
▶ To synthesise this information
▶ To interpret the synthesised information and form a conclusion about it

Step 1 Work on your skills

ACTIVITY 1

Answers

The problems puppies suffer	The problems horses suffer
their health and welfare is compromised	sinking and dying under crushing loads
genetic diseases	left without sustenance
painful abnormalities	starved to death
behavioural problems	forced to gnaw their own coats in the agonies of hunger
short life spans	

Check that students have grouped their information under the given headings.

Step 2 Practise your skills

ACTIVITY 2

This activity requires students to repeat the exercise in Activity 1 with a question worded slightly differently.

This activity is designed to test how closely they read the requirements of the question.

Again, check that students have grouped their information under the correct heading.

Step 3 Challenge yourself

This section of the unit encourages students to identify a text's purpose before analysing the techniques the writer uses in order to fulfil this purpose.

Unit 3 Synthesising information

ACTIVITY 3

Ask students what the purpose would be of:

- a charity letter telling you about the plight of children in a war zone?
- a leaflet about firework safety?
- an advertisement for a new theme park?

Make clear that the aims of a non-fiction text are seldom just to inform but often to instruct and persuade.

Students should familiarise themselves with the techniques often used in non-fiction texts, as given in the Student's Book:

- Strong, emotive language
- Facts
- Expert advice
- Personal pronouns
- Dramatic punctuation
- Pictures related to the text

Answers

	Example from Puppy Farming article	Example from Lord Erskine's speech
Strong, emotive language	'painful abnormalities'	'starved to death'
Facts	'200 breeding dogs'	'cruelty to animals is an offence.'
Expert advice	'go to a reputable breeder'	Lord Eskine has researched his speech, so the content can be considered expert advice.
Personal pronouns	'If you are thinking'	'they are forced to'
Dramatic punctuation	'200 breeding dogs on their farms!'	The use of a list, separated by commas, to stress the many cruelties horses suffer.
Pictures related to the text	'Sad dogs in cages'	

ACTIVITY 4

Make clear to students that they will need to identify and comment on the effect of these techniques in a **how** question, such as:

How do the writers convey cruelty to animals in these texts? [10]

You should comment on:

- **what** is said
- **how** it is said.

You must refer to the text to support your comments. Warn the students of the limited marks attained by just 'spotting' these techniques.

Answers

Suggested answers might be as follows, but reward all suitable answers.

	Example from Puppy Farming article	Example from Lord Erskine's speech	Effect the techniques have on the reader
Strong, emotive language	'painful abnormalities'	'starved to death'	Engages sympathy. Better answers will pick up on the striking adjective, 'painful', and evocative verb, 'starved'.
Facts	'200 breeding dogs'	'cruelty to animals is an offence.'	The extent of the problem shocks us. A warning is given in the speech that such cruelty is against the law.
Expert advice	'go to a reputable breeder'	Lord Eskine has researched his speech, so the content can be considered expert opinion.	The imperative, 'go to', and adjective, 'reputable', advise the reader. The social position of Lord Eskine and his factual speech leads us to trust the content.
Personal pronouns	'If you are thinking'	'they are forced to'	Direct address. 'They' and 'their' encourage empathy.
Dramatic punctuation	'200 breeding dogs on their farms!'	The use of a list, separated by commas, to stress the many cruelties horses suffer.	The exclamatory tone conveys shock. The frequent use of commas stresses the extent of animal cruelty.
Pictures related to the text	'Sad dogs in cages'		Encourages our sympathy.

Reading Units

Students can use the completed table to write up a full response to the question.

The P-E-E structure should be provided.

You may also wish to provide the following word banks.

For mid-achieving students:

Point
- The passage tells us,
- The passage continues,
- It goes on to say,
- We are also told,

Example
- Examiners prefer short quotes.

Explanation
- which tells us
- which shows us
- which illustrates
- which suggests

For higher ability students:

Point
- The idea of _____ is illustrated by…
- A sense of _____ is created in the phrase…
- This idea is exemplified by…
- This idea is furthered by…

Example
- Examiners prefer short quotes.
- High ability students should work to embed these.
- One-word quotes where the word class is identified, for example: 'The verb' starved' portrays…' are especially productive.

Explanation
- which conveys
- which portrays
- which illustrates
- which further presents
- which exemplifies
- which accentuates a sense of…

Tips

- Warn students to avoid the phrase, 'The passage quotes…' as neither writer here quotes from anyone else. This expression is a common error.
- Students often use the plural pronoun 'they' erroneously when describing a writer's style, for example: 'They tell us that…'. Remind students that an individual writer has written each text, not a group of writers.

The given question requires students to comment on the writers' techniques in both texts. A comparative approach is possible but students do not have to take this approach as the question does not ask for it.

Draw students' attention to the Top tips box on the correct use of comparatives.

BE EXAM READY

LEARNING OBJECTIVES

▶ To put the acquired synthesis skills into practice
▶ To practise these skills under timed pressure

Introduction

Recap on the skills acquired in this unit:

- Identifying the demands of an examination question
- Locating the information needed to answer it
- Synthesising the information and forming a judgement on its effect

Question 1

For this question, the advised time is:

- about 5 minutes reading
- about 40 minutes answering the questions

However, the actual GCSE examination timings will be a little longer (10 minutes reading, 50 minutes answering the questions) to reflect the longer extracts.

Answers

A4

1–2 marks	To those who identify and begin to comment on some examples of Byron's demands.
3–4 marks	To those who identify and give straightforward comments on the examples.
5–6 marks	To those who explain how a number of different examples convey the unusual nature of Byron's demands and link this to the idea that he is difficult to please. Students should begin to show some understanding of how language, tone and structure (but not necessarily all three) are used to achieve effects and influence the reader. These responses will begin to use relevant subject terminology accurately to support their comments.
7–8 marks	To those who make accurate comments about how a range of different examples convey Byron's demands and idiosyncrasies, and begin to analyse how language and structure are used to achieve effects and influence the reader. Subject terminology is used accurately to support comments effectively.
9–10 marks	To those who make accurate and perceptive comments about a wide range of different examples and their effects.

A5

Effectively, this question combines students' responses to **A2** and **A4**. The earlier questions implied that the writers held a negative opinion on celebrities' demands and this angle may have been partly addressed in students' earlier answers. However, question **A5** asks explicitly that students consider the writers' attitudes to celebrities.

These attitudes are negative. The marking guidelines for **A2** and **A4** can be used. Students' answers need not include a comparative element between the writers' approaches but may take this approach. They do not need to deal with each text equally but will not score over 6 if one text is dealt with almost exclusively.

The most thoughtful answers might point out that it is precisely the bizarre nature of celebrities' behaviour that interests us so much, and the fact that Medwin still wants to meet Byron, despite (maybe even because of!) his unusual character traits.

Comparing sample answers

Students should use the self-assessment criteria to mark the sample answers. You could distribute the examiner's commentaries below after they have done this.

Examiner's commentary – sample answer 1

- It is feasible that the writer doesn't like celebrities – there **is** a lot of negative language that could defend this approach, but it's a rather sweeping idea and is only substantiated by the explanation that they 'ask for weird things' with a few examples given.
- Referring to one writer as 'they' is a common student error.
- The first extract is dealt with almost exclusively, suggesting that the student didn't really understand the second one.
- This answer scores 2.

17

Reading Units

Examiner's commentary – sample answer 2

- This is a clear approach. The point that the writers are 'choos(ing)' certain information is a thoughtful one – this demonstrates an awareness of the writer's craft and that the reader is, perhaps, being manipulated.
- There is some specific reference to the text in the selection of appropriate quotation to support. The first writer's possible attitude to celebrities is presented through telling us that celebrities seem 'shallow and demanding', are 'fussy' and have 'too many demands'.
- The student has a go at language analysis.
- Medwin's attitude to Byron is neatly summarised with apt, if brief, textual support.
- There is some accuracy to the point that 'Byron sounds like he doesn't like anyone' although this isn't backed up with evidence and could be argued against as the text does cite that Byron has 'best friends' and 'his friend, Mr Shelley'.
- This answer scores 6.

Extension Activity

To extend this unit, students could go on to mark each other's answers.

This could be done anonymously in a future lesson so the teacher has time to cover students' names on the responses and copy a selection of exemplars.

When preparing your own mock papers, remember that sourcing 19th-century non-fiction extracts is likely to be more difficult than finding 21st-century references. A recommended approach is to source 19th-century extracts first, then find a complementary 21st-century text.

Unit 4
Types of information

LEARNING OBJECTIVES

▶ To identify different types of information – fact, opinion and bias
▶ To understand what a writer is trying to convey by using a certain type of information
▶ To understand why a writer uses a certain type of information

This unit focuses on preparation for Section A of Component 2 of the written examination: 19th and 21st century non-fiction reading. The time allocation for this section is 1 hour, comprising 10 minutes' reading and 50 minutes' writing. It is worth 40 marks – 30% of the qualification.

Candidates are assessed on their response to questions on two extracts (about 900–1200 words in total) of high-quality non-fiction writing, one from the 19th century, the other from the 21st century. This section of the exam assesses AO1, AO2, AO3 and AO4. The following unit deals with assessment objectives AO1 and AO2.

Assessment Objectives

AO1 ■ Identify and interpret explicit and implicit information and ideas.
AO2 ■ Comment on, explain and analyse how writers:
- use language (1a)
- use structure (1b)
- achieve effects (1c)
- influence readers (1d)
- using relevant subject terminology to support your views.

Introduction

It is worth noting that Eduqas may take the two Component 2 extracts from a number of different text types. These are listed in the specification as including letters, extracts from autobiographies or biographies, diaries, reports, articles and digital and multi-modal texts of various kinds from newspapers and magazines, and the internet.

Get going

Step 1 Work on your skills

ACTIVITY 1

Look for students to come up with definitions of fact and opinion like the following:
- A fact is something that we all agree is true and that can be confirmed.
- An opinion is belief; it is something believed to be true. Opinions can be held with confidence or conviction but cannot be backed up with absolute proof.

19

Reading Units

Answers

Statement	Fact or opinion?
Andy Murray is a Scottish tennis player.	Fact
Lionel Messi is the best football player of all time.	Opinion
Young people should do more exercise.	Opinion
Star Wars is the best film ever made.	Opinion
There are one hundred pence in a pound (£).	Fact
England won the World Cup in 1966.	Fact
Obesity is a growing problem in the United Kingdom.	Fact
Metallica are the best band of all time.	Opinion
Politicians should smile a bit more.	Opinion
Chickenpox is most common in children under ten.	Fact

Now, move onto superlatives.

Ask students what a superlative is and which of the statements in the above table are superlatives.

Extension Activity

Consolidate understanding with this quick activity.

Display or give students an incomplete version of the table below (which can be found on Dynamic Learning), asking them to fill in columns 3 and 4.

Text type	Extract from text	Positive or negative?	Effect
Charity leaflet	'This is the worst crisis to ever hit Sierra Leone.'	Negative	Shocks us. Encourages our sympathy.
Sports article	'The Tour de France winner has been called the greatest athlete on earth.'	Positive	Impresses us.
BMW advertisement	'The new BMW has the most innovative technology.'	Positive (worth pointing out to students that the word most could be used negatively with a different adjective after it)	Impresses us. Tries to persuade us to buy a BMW.

Step 2 Practise your skills

ACTIVITY 2

Answers

Facts (students to find three)	Opinions
Jay-Z has made millions.	Fans love his clothes.
Company founded in 1999.	Clothes appealed to everyone.
Reached annual turnover of $700 million.	Unique styling
His real name is Shawn Carter.	
He has profited from the company.	

The Student's Book explains the aim of the extract – to convey the popularity of the clothing line in a lively piece of writing.

Answers

How can you tell this?

- The language is very positive: 'popularity', 'appealed', 'unique'.
- Jay-Z is portrayed as very successful: 'Rap star', 'made millions', 'fans', 'profited'.

What is the effect of each technique used?

Technique used	Evidence from the text	Effect on the reader
Positive facts	'annual turnover of $700 million'	Makes the company sound extremely successful.
Language that makes the brand sound successful	'made millions', 'peak', 'profited'	The company has boosted Jay-Z's fortune – very successful.
Language that makes the brand sound popular	'Fans', 'love', 'popularity'	Jay-Z already has 'fans' – ready market. 'Love' – strong verb.
Vocabulary that might appeal to teenagers (the market for these clothes)	'rap star', 'urban style', 'styling', 'unique'	Teenagers will know Jay-Z's music – want to be a part of the rap culture.
A confident tone	'certainly'	The adverb emphasises Jay-Z's profit. Serves to make all the opinions sound like fact.

Unit 4 Types of information

Higher ability students may also identify that a downturn for the company is implied in the phrases:

- 'At its peak'
- 'At the height of its popularity'
- 'had an annual turnover'
- 'their styling was so unique'

but this downturn is not addressed. This idea is addressed in the exercise that follows in the Student's Book.

Next, read and discuss the exercise and information on bias. You may wish students to define bias before reading the explanation in the Student's Book.

Students should now be able to review the extract and tell that:

- there is fact, opinion and bias
- the writer is trying to convey a positive image
- this is done to try to make the reader regard the clothing line positively.

Step 3 Challenge yourself

ACTIVITY 3

This should be a full answer, structured as follows:

- Technique used
- Evidence from the text
- Effect on the reader

A self-assessment guide is provided in the Student's Book.

Extension Activity

This is a quick activity to consolidate understanding about facts and the effect they have.

Give students the following examples of opinions that are presented as facts. Ask students what the effects of these are.

Text type	Example	Effect
Charity leaflet	Reading Sam's story will make you realise how we need your help.	The case study probably will encourage the reader's sympathy but 'will make you realise' is opinion.
Advert for trainers	With revolutionary 'Max Lift' technology, the soles make you feel like you're running on air.	The imagery used promotes the comfort of the trainers but 'like you're running on air' is not a guaranteed outcome.
Council leaflet	The park is the most beautiful in the Gloucester area.	The superlative and adjective make the park sound attractive but 'most beautiful' is an opinion.

Improve your skills

LEARNING OBJECTIVES

▶ To identify main ideas and supporting ideas in a text
▶ To understand the difference between explicit and implicit meaning
▶ To understand how different types of information affect our understanding of a text
▶ To interpret this information and draw inferences from it

21

Reading Units

Step 1 — Work on your skills

ACTIVITY 1

You could provide a copy of the *The Guardian* extract below that students can highlight.

Two different coloured highlighters would be useful.
- The main points are shown here in **bold**.
- The supporting points are underlined.

These are open to discussion but any section that conveys extra information qualifies as a supporting point.

> **Six-year-olds understand digital technology better than adults**
>
> They may not know who Steve Jobs was or even how to tie their own shoelaces, but the average six-year-old child understands more about digital technology than a 45-year-old adult, according to an authoritative new report published on Thursday.
>
> **Children learn how to use smartphones before they are able to talk**
>
> The advent of broadband in the year 2000 has created a generation of digital natives, the communication watchdog Ofcom says in its annual study of British consumers. Born in the new millennium, these children have never known the dark ages of dial up internet, and the youngest are learning how to operate smartphones or tablets before they are able to talk.
>
> **Changing communication trends**
>
> 'These younger people are shaping communications,' said Jane Rumble, Ofcom's media research head. 'As a result of growing up in the digital age, they are developing fundamentally different communication habits from older generations, even compared to what we call the early adopters, the 16-to-24 age group.'
>
> For those aged 12 to 15, phone calls account for just 3% of time spent communicating through any device. For all adults, this rises to 20%, and for young adults it is still three times as high at 9%. Today's children do the majority of their remote socialising by sending written messages or through shared photographs and videos. 'The millennium generation is losing its voice,' Ofcom claims.

As reinforcement, you could try the exercise in the Top tips box on page 36 of the Student's Book.

ACTIVITY 2

Begin by explaining explicit and implicit meaning. An explanation is also given in the Student's Book.

Then, read the continuation of the article and have students answer the questions.

Suggestions are provided in the Student's Book.

Extension Activity 1

This whole-class activity can be used to consolidate understanding.

Write the following two sentences on the board. Ask students, as a class, to identify explicit and implicit understanding.

1 There is an average wait of 5–10 minutes for a New York subway train. In Hong Kong, it is 2 minutes.
  Explicit – the times differ.
  Implicit – the New York subway system is not as efficient as Hong Kong's.
2 1950s' teenagers did three times as much outdoor exercise as 21st-century teens.
  Explicit – 1950s teenagers did more exercise.
  Implicit – 21st-century teens are not as fit as 1950s' teens.

Extension Activity 2

First, have students read the Top tips box explaining when to use **affect/ed** and **effect**.

Then, write the following cloze exercise on the board, or distribute a copy to students (which can be found on Dynamic Learning), asking them to fill in whether to use **effect** or **affect**.

The answers are in bold.

1 The facts had a striking **effect** on me.
2 The bad weather will **affect** the runners.
3 The medicine had a terrible **effect** on him.
4 I was really **affected** by the news.

Unit 4 Types of information

Extension Activity 3

First, read the margin feature explaining how to use the word **impact** as a noun.

Write the following sentences on the board. In each, the word **impact** is used incorrectly. Ask students to rewrite each sentence so that it is correct.

This could be done by using 'impact' as a noun, by replacing 'impact' with the word 'affect/ed', or by completely rewriting the sentence.

1 I was really **impacted** by the news.
2 The facts **impact** the reader.

Example answers

1 I really felt **the impact** of the news. *or*
   The news really **had an impact** on me. *or*
   I was really **affected** by the news.
2 The facts **have an impact** on the reader. *or*
   The facts **affect** the reader.

Step 2 Practise your skills

Before beginning Activity 3, you could ask students to highlight the different types of information (main points or supporting points) in the dolphin 'superpod' extract.

Two different coloured highlighters would be useful.

Whole class or group discussion can encourage students to draw inferences and identify bias.

Main points	Supporting points
'Dolphin "superpod" spotted in Welsh waters	'"most spectacular" sighting in 10 years'
marine wildlife conservation charity Sea Trust	mile long wall of dolphins
Pembrokeshire	'30-mile stretch'
	'between Milford Haven and Lundy'
	superpods of common dolphin
	spotted by the charity 'Sea Trust'
	routine survey at the weekend
	Pembrokeshire waters
	'On three occasions'
	'most spectacular'

Main points	Supporting points
	'Cardigan Bay is a fantastic area to spot dolphins'
	'the UK's biggest pod of dolphins calling it home'

ACTIVITY 3

This activity asks students to put these pieces of supporting evidence in order of importance and justify their list.

Clearly, this is quite a subjective exercise and open to discussion but a similar pattern is likely to emerge.

Answers

Possible order:

1 Photographs. (These are noticed immediately.)
2 The report was able to say where the dolphins were seen. (This is stated in the main headline.)
3 The number of dolphins. (This is stated in the subheading.)
4 Quotes from a conservation group spokesperson. (This starts the main part of the article.)
5 Superpods have been seen before on three occasions. (4 and 5 may be interchanged – both are close to the start of the article.)

ACTIVITY 4

Answers

Explicit	Implicit
Over 1000 dolphins were seen off the Pembrokeshire coast.	We like dolphins.
The dolphins were seen somewhere between Milford Haven and Lundy.	Dolphins are a sign of healthy seas.
Such a large number of dolphins have never been seen before in this area.	It's a privilege to see them.
A conservation charity conducts surveys of dolphins quite often.	

ACTIVITY 5

You could begin by discussing the conclusions from Activity 4.

From the article we can infer that:

- dolphins are quite rare in British waters
- large numbers of dolphins are not often seen together
- the waters off the Pembrokeshire coast are reasonably clean and healthy.

23

Reading Units

Extension Activity

An optional writing task would fit well here.

Using the dolphin extract as stimulus material, students write a short newspaper piece (approximately 250 words) about the incident from an anti-dolphin viewpoint. Use the heading, 'Plague of dolphins destroying fishermen's livelihood'. Include quotes from fishermen. Remember to use bias in the words you choose. **[20 marks]**

Depending on the students' ability, you may wish to provide some or all of the following ideas.

Structural points

- Headline
- Subheadings
- First paragraph summarises story
- Quotes from those involved
- More detail as article progresses

Useful techniques

- Strong, emotive language
- Facts
- Expert advice
- Personal pronouns
- Dramatic punctuation

Note: The above conventions can be observed but writing in columns is not necessary and, with the resulting gaps, can actually make students think they have written more than they have.

Word bank

Adjectives	Nouns	Verbs	Adverbs
adverse	annoyance	affect	adversely
bothersome	dilemma	change	considerably
damaging	issue	control	desperately
detrimental	livelihood	disturb	dreadfully
difficult	nuisance	influence	extremely
problematic	plague	overcome	greatly
troubling	problem	pressurise	seriously
unmanageable	situation	upset	terribly

Sentence builders

Arguably   However   According to
Furthermore   Nevertheless   A powerful argument is
Likewise   Conversely   Statistics show that
Also   Contrary to this view   Many will agree that
Similarly   On the other hand   A consideration must be

Quote indicators

commented   pointed out   remarked   mentioned

> Remind students that they are unlikely to need the word 'quoted' as their interviewees are giving their own opinion, not quoting someone else.

Students who are unfamiliar with the formal writing style of newspapers tend to make the following errors:

- Using first person narrative: 'I interviewed a fisherman who told me...'
- Appealing directly to the reader: 'If you know anybody who...'
- Ending with a telephone number: 'Call us on...'

Assessment Objectives

AO5
- Communicate clearly, effectively, and imaginatively, selecting and adapting tone, style and register for different forms, purposes and audiences
- Organise information and ideas, using structural and grammatical features to support coherence and cohesion of texts.

AO6
- Candidates must use a range of vocabulary and sentence structures for clarity, purpose and effect, with accurate spelling and punctuation.

The total mark for the task (/20) will be given by awarding two marks in two different areas:

- communication and organisation (12 marks)
- vocabulary, sentence structure, spelling, punctuation (8 marks)

You can find the Eduqas mark scheme on the Eduqas website.

BE EXAM READY

LEARNING OBJECTIVES

▶ To identify and interpret fact, opinion, bias, inference, sub-text, main ideas and supporting ideas in a text
▶ To understand the effect of these types of information
▶ To explain why a writer uses these types of information

Introduction

Begin by recapping the skills acquired in this unit:

- identifying fact and opinion
- understanding the difference between main and supporting points
- understanding the difference between explicit and implicit meaning
- learning how to find 'hidden' meaning.

The aim of this section is to combine these skills in analysis of the text below.

Draw students' attention to the Top tips box and remind them that not all techniques are in every text. They should concentrate on analysing the techniques that **are** used.

Question 1

You could remind students of the P-E-E structure, if appropriate, here.

You could also provide the suggested word banks that were given on page 16 in Unit 3 of this book.

Students may wish to mark their own work or peer-assess a work partner's response.

A self-assessment guide to possible points is included in the Student's Book.

Sample answers

The sample answers are provided in the Student's Book. The commentary is only included here.

Students can mark the answers and teachers can then provide feedback.

Commentary on sample answer 1

This response is well structured. It engages with the question immediately and finds evidence to support its points, often presented as embedded quotation. Appropriate facts are found and interpreted as making us 'feel very sorry for her'. There is clear understanding of her character. The contrast between rich and poor is highlighted and the effect that this has on the reader is understood. It could be developed but is a clear, succinct response. To move higher, the answer would benefit from closer language analysis. This scores 7 marks.

Commentary on sample answer 2

This response covers everything indicated in the question guidelines. The candidate has worked through every bullet point, ensuring that each is addressed extremely thoroughly. There is close analysis of language and technique in order to support points. This scores full marks.

Unit 5
Explaining language

LEARNING OBJECTIVES

▶ To be able to understand why a writer has chosen certain words
▶ To be able to explain the effect of the words chosen

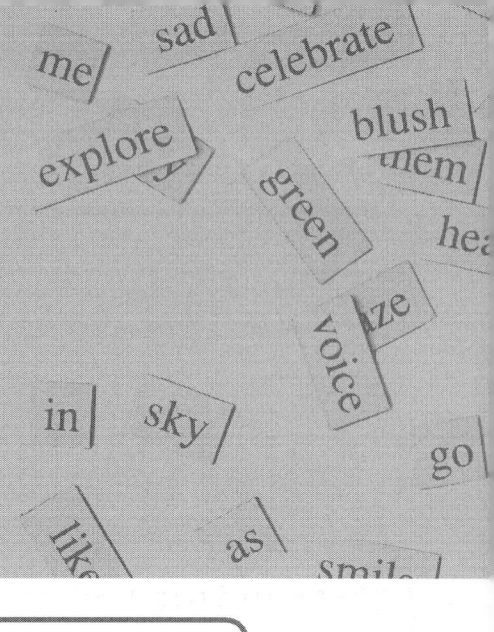

Assessment Objectives

AO2 ■ Explain, comment on and analyse how writers use language and structure to achieve effects and influence readers, using relevant subject terminology to support their views.
AO4 ■ Evaluate texts critically and support this with appropriate textual references.

Give students time to answer the 'How confident are you...?' table to establish their confidence at selecting and explaining key words and phrases and gauging prior learning.

Explain to students that they will often be expected to understand how a writer creates an impression of a character or a place. They will be expected to select language which helps to create these impressions. Tell them that in this section they will be learning about the P-E-E technique. Take students through the points relating to the P-E-E technique (see Unit 3 of the Teacher's Book).

Get going

Step 1 Work on your skills

ACTIVITY 1

Read the extract from *Tears of a Giraffe* and ask students to focus on the exam style question:
- What impressions do you have of the jeweller in this extract?

This can be an individual or a paired activity. Ask students to underline/highlight any words or phrases that tell them what the jeweller says and does in the passage.

Encourage students to work chronologically and methodically through the extract. Tell them that it is a good idea to work through the passage line by line to ensure that important information is not omitted or overlooked. They need to make sure they find points from the beginning, middle and the end of the extract.

Answers
- He is a good salesman.
- He is observant/nosy.
- He may be untrustworthy.
- He uses flattery.
- He is sneaky.
- He is prepared to embarrass Mr Matekoni.
- He is sexist.
- He knows the townspeople and all about them.
- He is a persistent salesman.

Next ask students, either individually or working in pairs, to find a quote or evidence from the passage to support each of the points they made in the previous activity.

Answers
Here are some of the quotes they may have found:
- He is a good salesman – 'He smiled at them.'
- He is observant/nosy – 'You parked your car under that tree.'
- He may be untrustworthy – 'The jeweller looked at him through his shifty eyes, and then glanced sideways at Mma Ramotswe.'; 'This is a clever man who cannot be trusted.'
- He uses flattery – 'You are a fortunate man'; 'Mr Maketoni acknowledged the compliment.'
- He is sneaky – 'And now you must buy her a very big ring'; 'A fat woman cannot wear a tiny ring.'

Unit 5 Explaining language

- He is prepared to embarrass Mr Matekoni – ' Mr Matekoni looked down at his shoes.'
- He is sexist – 'He seemed almost annoyed by her presence – as if this were a transaction between men and she was interfering.'
- He knows the townspeople and all about them – '"I know who you are," said the jeweller. "You can afford a good ring."'
- He is a persistent salesman – 'Here are some good diamond rings.'

Extension Activity

As an extension, encourage the students to write P-E-E style sentences using the points and evidence they have found.

This sentence could be used as a model/example for the students:

- The jeweller is a good salesman (point) because 'He smiled at them.' (evidence) This sentence suggests that he is welcoming because he is trying to encourage them to buy something. (explanation)

Students could be encouraged to label their own sentences initially until they become more confident. Also encourage students to use different sentence openings as shown in the Top tips box on page 45 of the Student's Book.

Spend some time collating and discussing these answers with them.

Step 2 Practise your skills

ACTIVITY 2

Explain to students that they will be building on and practising the same skills in this section of work. Read the extract from *Nice Work* with students and ask them to focus on the exam style question:

- What impressions do you have of the foundry? Ask students, either as individuals or in pairs, to underline/highlight the words/phrases used by the writer to create the impressions.

Go over their responses, perhaps as a whole class activity. Then, students should complete the table with Point-Evidence-Explanation to practise the P-E-E technique.

Possible answers

The foundry was not what Jane was expecting (point); 'even this warning did not prepare Jane for the shock of the foundry' (evidence); words like 'warning' and 'shock' sound dramatic and suggest how unprepared Jane is for what she sees (explanation).

The building was dark (point); 'a large building with a high roof hidden in gloom' (evidence); words like 'hidden' and 'gloom' create a negative and unpleasant atmosphere; 'gloom' suggests everything is dull, dreary and grey (explanation).

It was noisy (point); 'the place rang with the most barbaric noise Jane had ever experienced (evidence); the word 'rang' emphasises that the sound is assaulting her ears; the superlative terms 'most barbaric' suggest that Jane has never encountered such a sound in her life; 'barbaric' suggests there is a wildness and ferocity to the sound, as if it is almost hurting her senses (explanation).

Everything was unpleasant (point); 'the floor was covered in a black substance', 'grated under her shoes like sand' (evidence); the colour 'black' stresses how dark and dismal the surroundings are; 'substance' suggests a sense of mystery because Jane has no idea what she is stepping in!; 'grated' is a harsh, unnatural sound and stresses again how alien these surroundings are for Jane (explanation).

The smell was unpleasant (point); 'the air reeked with a sulphurous smell (evidence); the word 'reeked' suggests it is an unpleasant and bitter stench; 'sulphurous' suggests an acrid, disgusting smell (explanation).

There were extremes of heat and cold (point); 'shivering in an icy draught', 'frightening heat of a furnace on your face' (evidence); temperatures are not constant and extreme; 'shivering' and 'icy' suggest it can be freezing cold one minute and 'frightening' and 'furnace' describes unbearable and intense heat (explanation).

The mess was indescribable (point); 'everywhere there was indescribable mess and disorder (evidence); it suggests the scene was so chaotic and untidy that words cannot describe it (explanation).

Reading Units

Spend some time discussing and collating responses. Then encourage students to write their answer to the question using the information they have gathered and using the P-E-E technique. Students should be reminded to vary their sentence patterns by using the words/phrases in the Top tips box on page 45 of the Student's Book.

Step 3 | Challenge yourself

ACTIVITIES 3 AND 4

Read the extract from *Broken Homes* with the students. Focus their attention on the exam style question:

- What impressions does the writer create of the teacher and how are they created?

Encourage students, either as individuals or in pairs, to underline/highlight key words/phrases in the passage to help them answer the question. As with all the extracts they read in this unit, they should track through the passage methodically from the beginning to the end.

Remind them to try to think of an overview of their impressions at the beginning of their answer. They should use the P-E-E technique.

Next, read through the model answer with the students, drawing their attention to the good points and the use of the P-E-E technique. Then encourage the students to complete the answer as an individual task. When they finish, spend time listening to and going over responses.

Give students time to complete the 'How confident are you?' table to gauge whether confidence levels and learning have increased.

Improve your skills

LEARNING OBJECTIVES

▶ To practise explaining a writer's ideas and viewpoints
▶ To develop a secure approach to explaining the effect of the words chosen

Step 1 | Work on your skills

ACTIVITY 1

Focus students' attention on the exam style question:

- What impression does the writer create of Marcus's mum?

An initial approach could be to ask students, individually or in pairs, to come up with as many points as they can to help them answer the question. Here are some points they might make:

- She is 'weird' according to Marcus.
- She is responsible for him being weird.
- She just doesn't get it, any of it.
- She tells him that only shallow people make judgements because of clothes and hair.
- She discourages 'rubbish' and encourages reading.
- She prefers Joni Mitchell/Bob Marley to Snoop Doggy Dogg.
- She can explain why her taste is superior.
- She disapproves of Snoop Doggy Dogg's bad attitude to women.
- Marcus does admit 'it wasn't all his mum's fault'.

Spend some time collating and discussing responses.

Now ask students to write their own answer to the question. Remind them to include an overview and to use the P-E-E technique.

When they have finished, listen to and discuss answers.

Unit 5 Explaining language

Step 2 | Practise your skills

ACTIVITY 2

Ask students to underline the key words in the question.

Then, read the extract again and this time encourage them to underline/highlight details from the passage to help them answer the question. Remind them that this must be done in an organised and chronological way. Then encourage the students to find evidence from the text to match each impression they have found.

Tell the students to write their answer to the question in timed conditions – approximately 12 minutes. Remind them about the points in the Top tips box on page 48.

When they have finished, ask students to assess what they have written. Here are some points they might have decided to explore:

Overview:

- They have a close/fun relationship/they get on well.
- The key issue is the balance of power.
- His tone is ironic and often self-deprecating/he has mischievous sense of humour.
- He tries to present himself as the man of the house.
- He pretends to be rather condescending, treating her like a foreigner who doesn't understand local culture and for whom allowances have to be made.
- It turns out she is the boss/she only lets him go so far.
- She talks to him like an exasperated parent to a wayward child/humours him.
- She seems to know him only too well and she isn't impressed by his transparent attempts to charm her.
- She knows how to handle him/and to make him suffer!

More specific details:

- She usually does shopping for food/buys healthy food.
- He 'announces' that he is going to the supermarket because his wife keeps buying healthy food.
- He claims that she hasn't really grasped the 'spirit' of American eating.
- He thinks it is because she is British.
- He dashes around the supermarket like an excited child.
- She uses the special tone of voice with which she 'often addresses me in retail establishments' when he puts the box of Cookie Crisp in the trolley.
- He insists that she doesn't replace it with museli.
- She 'allows' him various forms of self-indulgence but with an obvious lack of enthusiasm.
- She eventually snaps.
- He tries to win her over, 'I beg your pardon my sweet'/'Isn't science wonderful?'
- She warns him that he will have to eat it all.
- He agrees in his 'sincerest voice'.
- And she makes him do exactly that!

Step 3 | Challenge yourself

ACTIVITY 3

This is an ideal opportunity for peer-/self-assessment. Ask students to tick every impression they have identified; then ask them to underline every piece of evidence used (there should be an equal number of ticks and underlining – each impression needs evidence).

They should check that each answer is focused with 'I think…' or 'I feel…'.

Spend some time discussing responses.

BE EXAM READY

LEARNING OBJECTIVES

▶ To adopt a confident approach to answering exam questions
▶ To feel confident about writing under timed conditions

Explain to students that they have already practised explaining the impressions a passage might give of a person, place or organisation and how these impressions are created by the way details and words are chosen by the writer.

Now they will have the chance to look at sample answers to exam questions, mark their own responses and write under timed responses.

Question 1

To begin, students could be asked to find the impressions and evidence and write them into a table (which can be found on Dynamic Learning).

Students should then be given approximately 12 minutes to write an answer to this question.

Encourage them to self- or peer-assess using the points in the Student's Book.

Spend some time collating and discussing responses.

Question 2

Students should aim to write their answer in approximately 12 minutes.

When they have finished, ask them to compare the points they have made and the evidence they have used with the points given in the self-assessment box.

Again, spend some time going over and discussing responses, perhaps in groups or as a class.

Explain to students that to improve exam technique and performance they will look at some sample answers to the same question.

When they have studied the sample answers, ask students to come up with the advice they would give to improve the responses.

- For sample answer 1 they might say that the answer is undeveloped and lacks evidence from the passage.

- For sample answer 2 they might suggest that the points need to be explained in more detail and that more evidence from the passage is needed. At this point some examples of P-E-E sentences could be modelled to emphasise the skills needed.
- For sample answer 3 they would probably agree that this is a very good answer.

Extension Activity 1

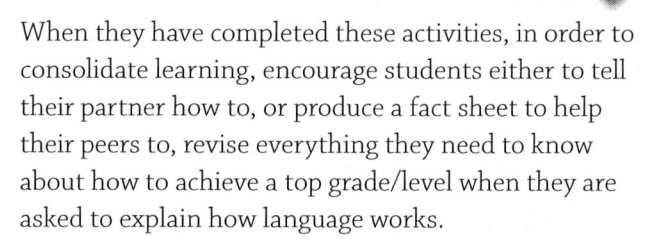

When they have completed these activities, in order to consolidate learning, encourage students either to tell their partner how to, or produce a fact sheet to help their peers to, revise everything they need to know about how to achieve a top grade/level when they are asked to explain how language works.

Give students some time to complete the '… do you think your confidence has increased?' table to assess whether they feel they are now more confident in these skill areas.

Extension Activity 2

Ask students to read this extract. It is from a novel which is set in Botswana, a country in South Africa.

> In Johannesburg they spent two weeks training us. We were all quite fit and strong but nobody could be sent down the mines until he had been made even stronger. So they took us to a building which they had heated with steam and they made us jump up and down on the benches for four hours each day. They told us how we would be taken down into the mines and about the work we would be expected to do. They talked to us about safety, and how the rock could fall and crush us if we were careless. They carried in a man with no legs and put him on a table and made us listen to him as he told us what had happened to him.

30

> They taught us Funagalo, which is the language used for giving orders underground. It is a strange language. There are many words for push, shove, carry, load and no words for love or happiness or the sounds which birds make in the morning.
>
> Then we went down the shafts. They put us in cages, beneath great wheels and these cages shot down as fast as hawks falling on their prey. They had small trains down there and they took us to the end of long, dark tunnels, which were filled with green rock and dust. My job was to load rock after it had been blasted and I did this for ten hours every day.

Students should focus on this exam-style question:

- What impressions do you get of work in the lines from this extract? You must refer to the text to support your answer.

Ask students to fill in the table below as preparation to help them answer the question.

Impressions	Evidence
	The miners were fit and strong but had to be made stronger.
	They were trained in a building heated with steam.
	They talked to us about safety and how rocks could fall.
	They brought a man with no legs to talk to us.
	We were taught Fungalo, a language for giving orders.
	Fungalo had no words for love or happiness.
	We were put in cages beneath great wheels.
	Tunnels were filled with green rock and dust.
	I did a ten-hour shift with no break.

Here are some possible answers they might think of:

- Suggests it would be hard work – Miners were fit and strong but had to be made stronger
- They need to be fit and have stamina – Trained in a building heated with steam
- They were informative and responsible, and it suggests it is dangerous – They talked to us about safety and how rocks could fall
- Shows the serious nature of job by including a very real example – They brought a man with no legs to talk to us
- Suggests they must follow instructions and commands – We were taught Fungalo, a language for giving orders
- Suggests harsh and cruel environment – Fungalo had no words for love or happiness
- They were treated like cattle/animals with no respect/prisoners who are trapped – We were put in cages beneath great wheels
- Dirty and unhealthy working conditions – Tunnels were filled with green rock and dust
- They work long, tiring hours – I did a ten-hour shift with no break

As an overview, students might write that the mine was harsh, horrible, grim and bleak.

To assess the students' responses, it may be helpful to think in terms of these broad areas;

0 marks	If the student hasn't written anything or doesn't engage with text and/or question.
1 mark	If the student makes simple comments with the occasional reference to the text, or if the student copies chunks of text unselectively.
2–4 marks	According to the quality, if the student makes simple comments based on surface features of the text and/or shows awareness of the more obvious implicit meanings. Better answers will begin to look at the issue of technique.
5–7 marks	According to the quality, if the student begins to select and makes valid comments/inferences based on appropriate detail from the text. Better answers will show some awareness of the writer's technique.
8–10 marks	According to the quality, if the student selects and analyses detail from the text showing insight into technique and the use of language. These answers should show overview and understand the writer's craft.

It is worth remembering that 'how' is partly a matter of content and partly a matter of language. The best answers take the 'extra step' to analyse the detail rather than spotting it.

Unit 6
Talking about language

LEARNING OBJECTIVES

▶ To understand how a writer makes a text interesting
▶ To be able to explain how writers use language and structure to make a text interesting

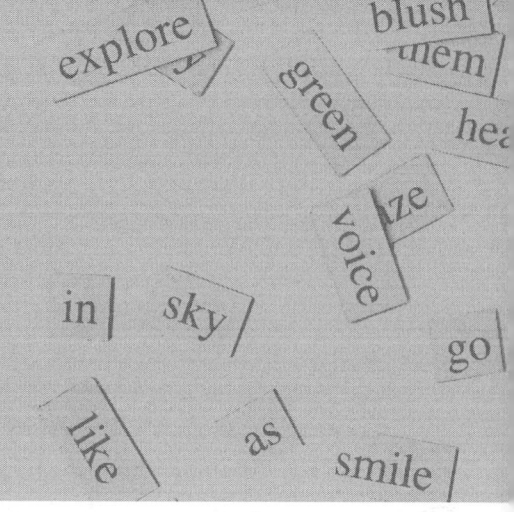

Assessment Objectives

AO2 ■ Explain, comment on and analyse how writers use language and structure to achieve effects and influence readers, using relevant subject terminology to support their views.
AO4 ■ Evaluate texts critically and support this with appropriate textual references.

Explain to students that when they read a text they will need to understand why it has been written and the intended purpose of the piece. Explain that they will also need to understand how the writer affects the reader and how the text is made interesting.

Get going

Step 1 Work on your skills

ACTIVITY 1

Students should read the article about the 'polar bear capital of the world' and then try to decide how the writer makes the article interesting.

Encourage them to read the article a second time with a partner and then, in pairs, to underline/highlight any words/phrases they find interesting.

Ask them, in pairs, to complete the table and say why each point is interesting. Here are some points they might make.

Evidence	Why it is interesting
Use of 'Help!'	Arouses interest with the suggestion of something dramatic; use of imperative suggests fear and use of exclamation adds to tension and sense of danger
Use of 'scare bear'	Use of rhyme suggests danger/excitement
Invasion of a large number of bears	Makes them sound dangerous and threatening, almost like an invading army that is coming to terrorise the inhabitants
Tone is informal and humorous	Engages the interest of the reader
Use of 'polar bear capital'	Attracts interest and gives impression it is an important place; also creates feeling of humour
First person viewpoint	Creates impression of immediacy and we share experiences of narrator; creates sense of realism
Writer unaware of dangers	Adds to humour but at the same time emphasises the potential danger and threat

32

Unit 6 Talking about language

Evidence	Why it is interesting
Tour guide snaps at him	Creates humour as writer is so inexperienced and clueless; could suggest frustration/exasperation she feels about tourists
Use of dialogue	Adds to sense of realism. Tour guide appears to be expert so we believe what she says because of her experience
Advice from the guide	Creates humour because it sounds so ridiculous but it is clearly true
Use of 'polar bear jail'	Creates humour; bears are almost personified and treated as dangerous criminals who must be locked up to protect the innocent inhabitants of Churchill
Use of statistics	Adds sense of realism to article and also underlines the potential danger of the situation
Emotive words/phrases	'invade' – makes them seem like a threatening enemy or army trying to take over the area; 'most dangerous predators on earth' – use of the superlative suggests nothing could be more threatening and frightening; 'predator' makes them sound as if they are hunting the inhabitants; 'Fast, strong and unpredictable' – tripling suggests their deadly qualities – power, speed and the fact that no one knows exactly how they will react; 'attack without warning' – reminds us of their deadly danger
Contrast between the look of the animals and their deadly potential	A reminder not to be taken in/deceived by them

Then encourage students to use the information they have gathered and the P-E-E technique.

If the class needs more help, you could model a sentence for the students to copy and then ask them to produce P-E-E sentences of their own for each of the points they have come up with.

Spend some time going over and discussing these with the class.

Step 2 Practise your skills

ACTIVITY 2

Read the article 'Going the Distance' with the students and explain that they will be focusing on the same skills of deciding how the writer makes the article interesting to read.

As before, encourage students to read the article once again with a partner and to underline/highlight words/phrases/techniques they have found interesting. They should aim to find at least seven points from the article and they should look for the corresponding evidence/details to support the points they make.

When they have gathered the points they want to make, students should write their own individual answer to the question.

Remind students that every sentence they write should gain credit otherwise there is no point in writing it!

When they have completed their answers, they can compare with the points suggested in the Student's Book.

This could be an opportunity for peer-/self-assessment. Encourage students to reflect on their response and to decide whether every sentence they have written is relevant and actually answers the question.

If they find they have not included enough evidence, they should go back to add this.

Step 3 Challenge yourself

ACTIVITY 3

Ask students, in pairs or individually, to read the three sample answers to the previous question. Encourage students to think about how each response could be developed and improved. Here are some points they might make:

Sample answer 1
Each sentence would earn credit/a tick; the answer spots some details but never moves into the realms of exploring 'how' the article is made interesting.

To improve the response, it needs to be longer; more details from the article need to be selected; the points need to be explained and explored more fully; language/key words need to be examined.

Sample answer 2
This response is more successful because it is longer and more developed. The first sentence, for example, is trying to probe the language and is beginning to consider how the article is made interesting. Some details are selected and there is a conscious attempt to look at how the writer uses language to make it interesting.

Reading Units

However, the response can still be improved by writing about details from the beginning, middle and the end of the extract.

Sample answer 3
This response is the most successful of the three answers because it is detailed and developed. This response considers the language used and the effects of the picture. The answer selects material effectively and methodically, and coverage of the extract is quite thorough.

Improve your skills

LEARNING OBJECTIVES

▶ To understand how a text presents the viewpoint and attitude of the writer
▶ To identify and write about bias

Explain to students that it is not always straightforward to work out and understand a writer's viewpoint. In order to become adept at doing this, they will need to read between the lines and develop their inference skills in order to work out the implied meaning.

You could introduce/revise the key terms here.

Also take students through the information in the Top tips box to help consolidate the techniques used in written texts.

Step 3 Work on your skills

ACTIVITY 1

a Remind students about emotive language and why this can be an effective technique. Ask students, in pairs or individually, to rank the list of adjectives in order from the least emotive to the most emotive. Here are the answers they might come up with:
- OK
- nice
- good
- wonderful
- superb
- bad
- disappointing
- frustrating
- dreadful
- appalling

Spend some time discussing answers and thinking about the connotations of each word.

b This can be a paired or individual task.

Ask students to consider what Peter Scudamore thinks about The Grand National race. They should pick out some of the emotive words that suggest this. Here are points they might come up with.

- 'I love the Grand National'/'I'll defend it to my last breath' – suggests his approval for the race; 'love' is a much stronger and more emotive word than 'like'; 'defend' suggests he is a staunch supporter.
- 'toughest horse race in the world' – suggests his admiration for the demands of the sport
- 'But even I can see that this year's race was agonising to watch' – suggests he is not blinkered or blinded to the pain and potential danger of the sport; shows a balanced viewpoint; shows an understanding of how other people might react to it

Spend some time collating and discussing possible answers. Then encourage students to write a paragraph in response to the question by using the P-E-E technique.

c Direct students to read article on seagulls. In order to help them organise and formulate their ideas they should copy and complete the table.

This could be a paired or individual task.
Here are some possible responses:

Evidence	Writer's opinion
Seagulls are thriving.	Suggests the problem of the seagulls is increasing
A list of damaging verbs, 'attacking', 'deafening', 'damaging', 'spreading'	Suggests they are aggressive, dangerous, hostile, threatening, noisy
They are 'huge' birds.	Suggests they are a force to be reckoned with and are capable of causing potential damage and injury
'hardened muscle'	They are strong and powerful/almost machine-like.
'vicious beaks and claws'	They are aggressive, nasty, threatening and violent; ready to attack.
'an army of greedy and aggressive birds'	This isn't the usual image of birds.
They have attacked humans.	Suggests they are not frightened of humans and see them as targets

Students should be encouraged to add more details to the grid. They might suggest the following words/phrases:

- spreading panic and disease
- a new urban menace
- they slash with their claws
- they are notorious

Unit 6 Talking about language

Extension Activity

Ask students whether these details suggest that the writer has a positive or negative opinion about the seagulls. They should realise it is a negative attitude!

Encourage them to produce a written answer to this question and then spend some time going over the responses.

Step 2 Practise your skills

Go over the Top tips box with the students and focus their attention on how to organise their response and structure their comments.

ACTIVITY 2

In order to consolidate and practise these skills, read the article 'Reinventing the Wheel' with them and consider the question that follows.

Encourage students to use this question as exam practice. Allow them approximately 12 minutes to complete their answer.

When they have finished, they can compare their responses with the points suggested in the Student's Book. Point out the advantages of an overview sentence at the start of each section to sum up the writer's attitude.

Use this as an opportunity for peer-/self-assessment.

Ask students to consider how well they have covered the extract and whether they have included details from each of the three different sections. Their answers should have remained focused throughout. Ask them to check that their sentences contain the phrases 'the writer thinks…' and 'the writer feels…'.

Step 3 Challenge yourself

ACTIVITY 3

Having read the essay 'is Fairtrade really fair?' students should attempt to write their answer in approximately 12 minutes.

When they have finished they should check they have covered the extract chronologically and methodically by choosing material from the beginning, middle and end. Every sentence should earn them credit or a tick. Every sentence should have the focus, 'the writer thinks…' or 'the writer feels…'.

Students could be encouraged to look at an exam-style set of criteria to award a mark for their response.

1 mark	If you made simple comments and occasionally selected detail from the text, or if you copied out parts of the text which are irrelevant to the question. You haven't really answered the question.
2–4 marks	If you made simple comments based on surface features of the text or showed awareness of more straightforward implicit meaning. Your answer may have been thin or brief or the details you selected from the text were not relevant to the question.
5–7 marks	If you selected appropriate detail from the text to show clear understanding of the writer's viewpoint/ideas.
8–10 marks	If you selected appropriate detail to sustain a valid interpretation. Your answer may have been be detailed, thorough, perceptive and have covered a range of points accurately and coherently.

BE EXAM READY

LEARNING OBJECTIVES

▶ To adopt a confident approach to answering exam questions
▶ To feel confident about writing under timed conditions

Question 1

Ask students to read the article 'The Lasting Resort' by Roy Hattersley and answer the following question in approximately 12 minutes.

Encourage students to give an overview of the writer's feeling before they start writing about the specific details in the article.

When they have finished, they can use their answer as an opportunity for peer-/self-assessment and compare the points they have included in their answer with the points given in the Student's Book.

Encourage students to reflect on their performance by checking that they have:

- included an overview or a general impression of the writer's opinion
- included points from the beginning, middle and end of the extract
- written sentences that are focused and relevant to the question
- taken a chronological and methodical approach to the extract
- included enough different points/details.

Question 2

Students should answer the exam-style question in approximately 12 minutes.

When they have completed their answer they can use it as an opportunity for self-assessment and compare it with the list of possible points given in the Student's Book.

Next, ask students to read the three sample answers to the same question and rank them in order from best to worst. (The order is 3, 1, 2.) They should be encouraged to think how each answer could be improved.

Extension Activity 1

Ask students to read the following article by Adam Edwards from the *Telegraph*.

The Rise and Fall of Mr Fox

It is hard to believe that an animal so blessed as Mr Fox could so casually have chucked away his burnished image. Yet this summer he managed to do just that.

In 2010, he bit and mauled baby twins as they slept in their cot in London. And suddenly it dawned on the urban population of Britain that Basil Brush had a beastly side. He was nothing more than a feral chav, breeding indiscriminately and feeding off buckets of KFC.

Last month, it was revealed that he had crept into London Zoo and killed 11 penguins. For fun. Worse still, he decapitated the Queen's flamingos at Buckingham Palace and killed a number of pet rabbits, owned, unfortunately for him, by the children of various newspaper writers who then let rip in print.

It has not deterred him, and the charge sheet grows weekly: a woman in Fulham had her ear savagely bitten while sleeping in her bedroom. A baby boy was attacked in Dartford. In Islington a young girl had her arm mauled as she slept.

Across London, cries for the curbing of Reynard are mounting. Some have called – presumably in jest – for urban hunts to be introduced. It is hard for anyone in the countryside not to take pleasure in the misfortunes of the townies, particularly if you were one of the half million who demonstrated against the ban on fox hunting.

Unit 6 Talking about language

> Actually, the only surprise in the fox's recent reversal of fortunes is that he was ever thought of as lovable in the first place. His cunning was first noted in the Bible and in European folklore he has always symbolised trickery and deceit. In children's literature he rarely emerges with any credit. Even when the fox is a hero, as in Roald Dahl's *Fantastic Mr Fox*, he is also seen as a thief.
>
> The events of 2010 are proof that the urban fox is more fearless than ever and there is no immediate solution to the problem. Shooting is the most effective form of control, but it is of limited practical use in towns and generally unpopular with local people. As a result, many councils have given up trying to control the fox at all.

Students should attempt to answer the following questions in approximately 12 minutes.

How does Adam Edwards feel about foxes?

You should track through the article and think about:

- what he says
- how he says it.

Here are some of the points students might come up with:

Overview:

- He undermines the lovable image of the fox.
- He demonises the fox.
- He uses a lot of examples/anecdotes/lists.
- He uses emotive language.

Specific details/points:

- He claims that the fox has 'casually' thrown away his 'burnished image'.
- He reminds the reader of the attack on the baby twins.
- He claims people realised that the 'lovable' fox had a 'beastly side'.
- He brands him as a 'feral chav'.
- He brands him as an animal who breeds indiscriminately and eats discarded KFC.
- He lists the fox's crimes (very specific examples including attacks on children and pets).
- The fox is accused of killing for fun.
- Words such as 'mauled' and 'savagely' are used to demonise the fox.
- Large numbers opposed the ban on fox hunting (not everyone loves foxes).
- He uses the history of the fox in the Bible, in folklore and literature to remind us of its reputation as a cunning thief.

Extension Activity 2

Ask students to read the following article by John Humphrys.

> ### 'WASTE NOT, WANT NOT' – The Proverb We All Forgot
>
> In the wilds of Texas I once went to a restaurant called the Big Texan Its name derives partly from the size of the waiters – you have to be at least 6ft 6in to work there – and partly from the size of the portions. The speciality of the house is a steak that weighs 72oz. That is approximately the size of the average Sunday joint, with enough left over at least for another family meal.
>
> The appeal of the place is that if you eat the whole thing, including trimmings, starter and pudding, you get the meal for free. Pinned proudly to the wall is a list of all those who have succeeded in this great challenge. It included an 8 year old boy, a 76 year old grandmother and a builder who ate two.
>
> Most people give up and what they leave is, of course, thrown away. The whole place is one great temple to the worship of waste and if you ever feel the need for a swift dose of British moral superiority, I strongly recommend a visit to the Big Texan. When it comes to waste, the Americans are the unquestioned champions of the world.
>
> But the British are beginning to challenge them. An official report has revealed that we waste 500,000 tons of food every year. Now that is not food that has grown mould in the back of the fridge and lurks there threatening to take over the world; it is edible food that has merely passed its sell-by date on the supermarket shelves.

Reading Units

> It is worth about £400 million and it costs another £50 million just to get rid of it. Here is what happens to most of it.
>
> When we buy our food in the supermarket we rummage around on the shelves to find the product with the latest sell-by date. The stuff with the earliest dates is left on the shelf and, because the barmy rules and regulations would have us believe that we shall die in agony if we eat a spoonful of yogurt 30 seconds after the date on the carton, it ends up in the landfill site. It is shameful nonsense. Every year a typical supermarket chucks out 50 tons of perfectly good food. Still feel so smug about the wasteful Americans?
>
> The food could be used by any number of needy people, but we throw it out. Only a fraction is handed over to charities, who are constantly begging for more. Some of us might cluck a little over the wickedness of a world in which we waste food while Ethiopian children starve, but we get over it. We smile at memories of our mothers telling us it's wrong not to eat all your dinner when children are starving in Africa. The truth is, we only care about waste in the context of money. Our attitude seems to be, if we can afford to waste things, then why the hell shouldn't we?
>
> I'm still smarting from an interview I did last year. I confessed to the interviewer that I turned off lights when I left the room and boiled only a mug-full of water if that was all I needed. Could this really be true? I'm afraid so, I said. Such ridicule was heaped on me in her article that I bought all the papers in my local shop, dumped them in the recycling bin and went into hiding. If only I had admitted to being a serial murderer instead.

Students should consider the following sample responses to this exam style question:

How does John Humphrys present his attitude about being wasteful? [10]

Students should read the sample responses, rank them in order from the best to the least successful and think about how each one could be improved.

Sample answer 1

John Humphrys doesn't like the fact that we are so wasteful because he uses facts and figures. He says how we waste 500,000 tons of food every year. He also tells us how much money is wasted on food we buy in supermarkets — £400 million, and how much it costs to get rid of that food — £50 million. The article is written humorously and this makes it more interesting. He talks of the Americans because they are well known for obesity and wasting food. Then he compares the British to them, which can make us realise how bad the situation is and how much food we do waste. He reminds us about poor countries and the charities that need food. The use of headlines 'Waste Not, Want Not' is direct and straight to the point. It tells us not to waste the food we don't want. Underneath the title 'The Proverb We All Forgot' reminds us that we don't want to think about how much we waste.

Sample answer 2

John Humphrys shows us he is against wasting food because he tells us he would rather die than waste food that is perfectly fine and would be eaten by needy people. He tells us in a way which makes us feel ashamed if we do waste food. He uses phrases like 'still feel so smug about the wasteful Americans?' He show us it is a sin to waste food when people are starving to death in third world countries but in reality he is only proving that we waste a ridiculous amount of perfectly good food and he is right in what he says that it is still edible after its sell-by date.

Sample answer 3

> John Humphrys is shocked, appalled and embarrassed by the amount of food we waste each year. A point he makes early on in the article is 'if you ever feel the need for a swift dose of British moral superiority' then we should chuckle at the wasteful Americans he mentions, who are the 'unquestioned world champions' when it comes to waste. Then he successfully challenges the reader's sense of superiority. He begins with a short sentence, 'but the British are beginning to challenge them'. A bit later he asks the rhetorical question, 'still feel so smug about the wasteful Americans?' He presents facts that will catch the reader's attention and then debunk the reader's attitudes. For instance, he tells us the statistics that £400 million's worth of food wasted and that it costs £50 million to remove it. The 'Proverb We All Forgot' suggests that old wisdom, or common sense, as proverbs are often both, has been lost somewhere.

Students should identify that Sample answer 3 is the most successful; Sample answer 1 is next; Sample answer 2 is least successful.

Students might comment that Sample answer 3 is detailed and thoughtful with good coverage of the text. This would probably score 9.

Sample answer 1 handles use of statistics well and uses the comparison with USA; it has a steady and sensible approach but the comments are not always sharp. It is clearly engaged with the question and although it misses some points, there is evidence of purposeful selection. This would probably score 7.

Sample answer 2 is relatively brief with only limited engagement with the question. It is quite a thin response which drifts into personal views. This would probably score 3 or 4.

Unit 7
Analysing language

LEARNING OBJECTIVES

▶ To recognise a range of techniques and their effect
▶ To write effectively about what is said (content) and how it is said (the techniques used by the writer)

Assessment Objectives

AO2 ■ Explain, comment on and analyse how writers use language and structure to achieve effects and influence readers, using relevant subject terminology to support their views.
AO4 ■ Evaluate texts critically and support this with appropriate textual references.

Explain to students what the word 'analyse' means and how they will need to approach exam questions which require them to write about how a writer creates effect.

Get going

Step 1 Work on your skills

ACTIVITY 1

Individually or in pairs, ask students to read the list of statements and decide whether they provide a clear and precise explanation or whether they are too general and could be applied to any text. Here are the suggested answers:

The headline is big and bold and stands out.	vague
The words grab the reader's attention.	vague
The rhetorical question in the heading immediately draws the reader in by making him/her think about his own behaviour.	precise
The writer makes the reader want to read on.	vague
The writer uses interesting words to make us think.	vague
The writer uses emotive language such as 'agony' to make us feel sympathy for the animals.	precise
The subheading emphasises the worrying consequences and dangers caused by the hurricane.	precise
The use of alarming statistics highlights the scale of the problem of childhood obesity	precise

Go over responses and discuss the reasoning behind students' decisions.

Draw the students' attention to the Top tips boxes and encourage them to use these as a checklist for their own responses.

Also remind students that the language in headlines, headings and/or subheadings is important and needs to be considered carefully.

ACTIVITY 2

Ask students to work through this activity either individually or with a partner.

Students should study each headline in turn, underline the words/techniques they think would affect the reader in some way and then explain the effect of the language/techniques. Here are some points they might make:

- Headline 1
  - 'We' suggests a sense of collective unity and responsibility.
  - 'only stop' makes the reader feels guilty if they don't support the cause – a case of emotional blackmail.

Unit 7 Analysing language

- 'slaughter' is a dramatic and emotive word which sounds ferocious and barbaric and is designed to shock and appal the reader.
- 'innocent dolphins' makes them sound defenceless/vulnerable/helpless and is a sharp contrast with the word 'slaughter'.
- 'your help' again guilt trips the reader.
- Headline 2
  - 'Braving' sounds as if the lifeboatmen were selfless and heroic – almost superhuman.
  - 'Daring Rescue' shows how challenging the conditions were and how dedicated and professional the men were.
  - 'once-in-a-career' suggests no one had ever experienced such extreme conditions before and probably never would again.
  - 'haul' implies how strenuous and physically demanding the rescue actually was.
  - 'dangerously listing' suggests time was of the essence as the ship could capsize at any moment.
  - 'heaving sea' implies the wildness and ferocity of the weather conditions.
  - 'in the middle of the English Channel' suggests the bleakness of the situation and how exposed they all were.
- Headline 3:
  - 'Conqueror of the World' suggests the boy is powerful and heroic/almost superhuman?
  - The age of the boy is emphasised to show how remarkable his achievement is: 'Cabin Boy', 'teenager', 'youngest person'.

Spend some time collating and discussing responses.

Draw students' attention to the list of alternative words in the Top tips box to show how a writer tries to influence a reader.

Step 2 Practise your skills

ACTIVITY 3

Either individually or in pairs, students should study the headline and opening section from a leaflet encouraging readers to give blood.

They should then read the student response, which explains the effects of the headline and the language used. Ask students whether they think the response is successful.

Students should point out that the comments are vague and generalised. Although some key words have been selected, they have not been explained or commented on in any way.

Encourage students to explain better how the headline encourages readers to give blood.

Here are some points that could be made:
- The colour red is dramatic and symbolises the blood.
- Red is also the colour of danger and perhaps suggests people's lives could be in danger unless the reader is willing to give blood.
- The word 'do' is a command/order/imperative which suggests the writer is telling the readers that they have to give blood.
- 'amazing' is a dramatic and emotive adjective. It flatters the readers and makes them feel special and important if they do what they are told to do.
- 'today' makes the situation desperate and urgent as if there is no time to waste.
- The ellipsis (…) makes it sound dramatic and builds up tension as the readers realise that even they can do this.
- 'practically anyone can' suggests the readers don't have any excuse for not donating blood.

Spend some time collating and discussing possible responses.

Students should then continue their answer by focusing on the remaining paragraph of text. Here are some points they might make:
- 'Becoming a blood donor is really very simple' suggests they want the readers to feel reassured and comfortable instead of nervous and apprehensive.
- The use of 'you' and 'you're' makes the readers feel as if the leaflet is speaking to them personally and so makes them feel important and special.
- The word 'needs' suggests the Blood Service is desperate to receive more blood and there is an urgency about their appeal.
- The figures, 'nearly two and a half million', and statistics sound impressive and knowledgeable but at the same time they are also alarming.
- 'But only 6% of the UK population who are currently eligible, do so…' is a frightening fact and is designed to make the readers feel guilty if they ignore this appeal.

Step 3 Challenge yourself

ACTIVITY 4

Explain to students that the same skills and techniques can be applied to any piece of writing and then read with them the extract from *Tales of a Troubled Land*.

Focus on the exam-style question which draws attention to what happens to make Mike frightened; how the writer uses language to show he is frightened; how it makes the reader feel.

To help organise their ideas and to encourage them to adopt a methodical and chronological approach, they could complete the table either individually or in pairs. Here are some points they might make:

Reading Units

Evidence	Comment
'He was facing death'	He is convinced that he is about to be killed; suggests he is feeling cornered, trapped and very fearful.
'why should he have to die like this when he had always been hardworking and honest?'	He thinks about the unfairness of life.
'He lifted the heavy stick and brought it down on the head of his pursuer'	His fear made him act with unusual ferocity.
In a panic he runs 'wildly'.	Suggests his fear and shock at what he has done. It suggests he has lost control.
'ran into the side of an old lorry which sent him reeling'	It suggests how his panic and fear are making him clumsy.
He expects the blow that will kill him.	He is anticipating death as if it is inevitable.
'even then his wits came back to him'	His instinct for self-preservation makes him act.
'His stomach seemed to be coming into his mouth'	He is almost sick with fear.
'His heart thumped wildly in his chest'	He struggles to keep quiet and still.
'He tried to calm it down, thinking it might be heard'	He thinks he will give himself away or they will discover him because of the noise he makes.

Spend some time collating answers. Then encourage students to write a full answer to the question using the P-E-E techniques they have practised in earlier units.

This could be used as an opportunity for peer-/self-assessment. Students should decide whether every sentence they have written is focused and actually answers the question.

Ask them whether they have used evidence from the extract to prove every point they have made. In order to check that they have included sufficient evidence/explanation, encourage them to put a tick against every point they have made and underline every piece of evidence/explanation they have given.

Spend some time going over and discussing answers.

Improve your skills

LEARNING OBJECTIVES

▶ To practise writing about how effects are created
▶ To develop a secure approach to analysing language

Inform students that this section will build on the skills they have already developed by answering a range of questions and looking at sample answers.

Step 1 Work on your skills

ACTIVITY 1

Ask students what Bill Bryson's opinion is of the guesthouse. They should realise he has very negative feelings towards it!

Students should then focus on how Bill Bryson communicates his feelings to the reader.

To help them answer this question, encourage them to focus their reading by underlining the details from the passage that could be included in their answer.

Then reveal the list of possible details they could have chosen in the Student's Book so they can compare these with their own responses. Remind them about the importance of beginning their answer with an overview.

Ask them to read the list of possible overview statements and encourage them to select the most appropriate. They will probably decide on the following:

- It is tacky and dreadful.
- It is expensive for what it is.
- It seems dirty, neglected and uncomfortable.

Next, ask students to read the sample answer to this question and to write down two good things about the response. They might come up with the fact that it contains 11 references from the text; they might comment on the fact that the opening sentence gives an overview.

Then, ask students to write down two things that could be done to improve the response.

Unit 7 Analysing language

They might comment on the following:
- Some sentences are general and tend to state the obvious 'he creates the atmosphere mostly using language'.
- The comments need to be more specific and focused.
- Although details are selected, the words and their effect are not explored.

Select one sentence and model it to show students how to rewrite and improve it. Then encourage students to select two sentences of their own choice from the sample answer to rewrite/improve. Spend some time collating and going over responses.

Step 2 Practise your skills

ACTIVITY 2

Explain to students that they will be using the same skills for this activity.

Read the extract from *The Forgotten Enemy* with the students. Ask them to think about the question that follows.

To help them practise tracking the passage in a methodical and chronological way, encourage them to complete the table by commenting on the effect of the evidence that has been selected from the passage. Here are some possible points they might make:

Evidence	Comment
The momentary pause 'almost cost him his life'.	Suggests there is a sense of immediate drama/suspense/tension.
Something huge and white appears suddenly.	The reader is left to guess exactly what it could be/information is deliberately withheld from the reader to create tension/drama.
His mind refuses to accept the reality of what he sees.	Creates an intriguing effect as it suggests a clear sense of danger but still the information is withheld.
He fumbles desperately for his futile revolver.	Creates a sense of urgency in the language and therefore fear, but also 'futility' suggests real danger.
The polar bear is 'huge'.	Suggests it is clearly a very dangerous animal.
He drops his belongings and runs.	Suggests his desperate attempt to escape and 'floundering' suggests panic.
The station is only a few feet away.	Creates drama/tension as the reader wonders whether he will be able to reach safety in time.
He cannot hear his pursuer.	Is another example of all the predictable elements in a tense/dramatic 'chase' scene.
The temptation to look back is 'intolerable'.	Shows how terrified he is and this adds to the drama of the situation.

Evidence	Comment
The gates resist and this is a 'frightful moment'.	Creates tension as the reader begins to feel that everything is against him and that he will not escape.
They open 'reluctantly' and he 'forces his way in'.	Adds to the drama/tension because the narrow escape is just in the nick of time.
The bear is described as 'monstrous'.	Emphasises its size and the threat it poses.
It attacks the gates in 'baffled fury'.	Creates tension as the reader realises that the bear won't give up.
It 'slashes' at the rucksack as it retreats.	Emphasises what a close shave and lucky escape it was.

Draw their attention to the information in the Top tips box about how bullet points in the exam question may help them to organise their answer.

Step 3 Challenge yourself

ACTIVITY 3

Ask students to read the two sample answers to the exam-style question in Activity 2 and encourage them to decide which is the more successful response.

Hopefully they will realise that Example A is the more accomplished response. Ask them to think about what makes Example A a good answer. They might notice that it tracks the extract carefully; comments are always clear and purposeful; quotations are selected, used and commented upon neatly.

Ask students to imagine they were the examiner and to think about what sort of comment they might make about each response.

Example A

They might make the following comments:
- The response is well focused and answers the question.
- Every sentence would earn credit.
- Nothing is wasted.
- The response keeps to the text.
- The quotations are well chosen,
- There is good coverage of the extract.

Example B

They might make the following comments:
- The response is brief and undeveloped.
- The comments are vague and not specific.
- Quite a few of the sentences are meaningless/do not saying anything and so do not gain credit.
- Coverage of the extract is limited.
- Few words are commented on.

Reading Units

Spend some time listening to responses from students. Ask students how they could improve the following comments:

- The language is strong.
- The writer uses a lot of full stops and commas to create short and medium length, dramatic sentences to build suspense and tension.

Go over their suggestions.

Students should now write their own answer to the question and then reflect upon their own performance. Encourage them to answer the following checklist:

- Did they use a quote to support each point made?
- Did they earn credit for every sentence?
- Did they make at least six separate points?
- Did they track through the extract chronologically and methodically?

BE EXAM READY

LEARNING OBJECTIVES

▶ To adopt a confident approach to analysing language and effects
▶ To feel confident about structuring an answer under timed conditions

Explain to students that this section will provide them with an opportunity to use the skills they have been practising under timed conditions.

Question 1

Give students a copy of the article by Petronella Wyatt and the question, 'How does Petronella Wyatt get across to you what it is like to ride the TT course?'

Ask students to write their answer to the question in approximately 12 minutes (the time they will have in the exam). When they have finished, reveal some of the points given in the Student's Book that they might have included in their answer.

Encourage them to reflect on what they have written. Did they:

- find a quote to support each point made?
- earn credit for every sentence written?
- track through the extract chronologically and methodically?
- include details from the beginning, middle and the end of the extract?

Show them the mark scheme in the Student's Book and encourage them to award their answer a mark out of 10. Ask them to write down what they need to do to improve their performance next time. Go over responses. These should be used as targets for their next practice.

Question 2

Explain to students that they will be using the same skills to tackle the next activity.

Ask them to study the sample answers to this response and to mark them as if they were an examiner. Encourage them to find every point that deserves credit and evidence to support each point. Ask them to think about what advice they would give to improve each response.

- They might think that Sample A is a bit unclear and does not show complete understanding of what is going on. Coverage of the extract is a bit limited.
- They might think that Sample B covers the extract methodically and tackles some of the difficult points in the passage. Comments are insightful and clear and the text is used purposefully and selectively.
- They might think that Sample C is a bit uneven – there are some good points but the quality is not consistent throughout. There are some vague comments and assertions. The coverage is not very methodical but it does make some valid points.

Ask students to rank the answers in order from best to least successful. They should arrange them in this order: Sample B; Sample C; Sample A.

Now ask the students to write their own answer to the question in 12 minutes.

Extension Activity

Give students a copy of the following passage by Alexander McCall Smith which is set in Botswana, a country in southern Africa.

> I would have stayed in the mines. I suppose, had I not witnessed a terrible thing. It happened after I had been there fifteen years. I had been given a much better job, as an assistant to a blaster. They would not give us blasting jobs, as that was a job the white men kept for themselves, but I was given the job of carrying explosives for a blaster. This was a good job and I liked the man I worked for.
>
> He had left something in a tunnel once – his tin can in which he carried his sandwiches – and he had asked me to fetch it. So I set off down this tunnel where he had been working. The tunnel was lit by bulbs, but you still had to be careful because here and there were great galleries which had been blasted out of the rock. These could be two hundred feet deep and men fell into them from time to time.

Reading Units

> I turned a corner in this tunnel and found myself in a round chamber. There was a gallery at the end of this and a warning sign. Four men were standing at the edge of the gallery and they were holding another man by his arms and legs. As I came around the corner, they threw him over the edge and into the dark. The man screamed something about a child. Then he was gone.
>
> I stood where I was. The men had not seen me yet, but one turned around and shouted out in Zulu. Then they began to run towards me. I turned and ran back down the tunnel. I knew that if they caught me I would follow their victim into the gallery. It was not a race I could let myself lose.

Students should think about the following question:

How does the writer make these lines tense and dramatic?

Depending on how much help the students need at this stage, here are a few activities for them to work through.

They could be given the following table to complete – some of the boxes could be covered (see Dynamic Learning), again depending on the level of scaffolding required. This is the completed grid.

He tells us he witnessed a 'terrible thing'.	This builds tension by revealing that something very dramatic is about to happen although no details are given yet.
It makes him leave the mine.	This suggests it must be serious as he had only just got a better job.
He is working with explosives.	Here the author is laying a false trail by suggesting there could be an explosion.
The tunnel is lit but he says it still needs care.	This is tense because it hints at potential danger.
The galleries are very deep and men fall into them.	A sense of the ominous is developing and the warning sign reinforces this.
He encounters four men on the edge of one of the galleries.	This creates tension as it is an unexpected meeting.
They are holding a man over the edge of the gallery.	There is obvious tension here as the reader grasps what they are doing.
Obed sees them throw the man over the edge.	This is tense as he has witnessed a brutal and horrible murder.
The man 'screams something about a child'.	This is dramatic because it is emotional and horrific.
He then disappears.	This creates tension with the stark finality of 'then he was gone'.
Obed is not spotted at first.	This creates tension because he could get away.
Then he is spotted and chased.	This is dramatic because of the obvious tension of the 'chase'.
He knows he will be killed if he is caught.	This creates tension because of the drama of the 'life or death' chase.
He says it is a 'race' he could not afford to lose.	This creates tension because it points out exactly what is at stake.

Here are some sample answers for students to read and rank in order from best to least successful.

Answer 1

Obed had just finished saying how he wouldn't mind spending a longer period of time in the mines because he wasn't given dangerous jobs to do and he liked the man he worked for. His attitude to working in the mines changes dramatically as he realises there is more behind the story than he thought. The writer uses short sentences which make everything that Obed says bold and sharp. Tension builds more and more as you read these lines which makes the extract more dramatic. Reading the extract allows me to be able to imagine what Obed sees and hears as the text is very imaginative. Although the writer only briefly says what Obed sees, it has a big effect on the reader because it shows that maybe working in the mine isn't always a good idea and there is more to the story told. At the end the writer leaves the extract on a cliffhanger and makes you want to read on. Overall the writer makes it very tense and also makes it very addictive to read.

Unit 7 Analysing language

answer 2

The writer makes these lines tense and dramatic by the use of lexical choice, punctuation ad sentence construction. Firstly the lexical choice is key for creating tension and drama as words used like 'terrible' and 'screamed' give us the idea that something exciting is happening. This makes the reader want to read on as we want to know what happens. By this method the author has got our attention by using lexical choice or word choice he has created tension and excitement. Secondly by the punctuation or grammar he can create tension. By this the writer uses comma linkage, he puts sentences in parenthesis to make it seem as if the action is getting quicker and therefore more dramatic. Finally the way in which the writer can create tension and excitement is by sentence construction. Sentence construction is important as it gives the reader an idea that we are witnessing something that is really exciting. By making the sentences shorter and therefore quicker we are given the impression that this is exciting. I stood where I was. This sentence as an example is short and quick and gives us the indication that Obed is in trouble and that something dramatic is going to happen. Overall, a combination of all these give us as the reader enough information to make us think that a tense and dramatic scene is happening.

answer 3

The writer makes these lines tense and dramatic in many ways. Firstly he uses short sentences to increase the rhythm of the text. 'I would have stayed in the mines, I suppose, had I not witnessed a terrible thing.' This increases the rhythm which causes dramatic effect and tension is built because we want to find out why he left. He explains how he 'had been there fifteen years' and explains how he 'had been given a much better job'. This helps to cause tension because we want to find out what terrible event made him leave this better job. Then the writer explains how he witnessed a murder and the events after. 'Four men standing at the edge of this gallery and they were holding another man by his arms and legs'. This causes dramatic effect because we know that these galleries can be 200ft deep. It makes us want to read on to find out what they are doing. To increase drama and tension the writer uses short sentences at the time of the murder, 'As I came round the corner, they threw him over the edge into the dark. The man screamed something about a child. Then he was gone'. This brings the drama and tension to a climax with him witnessing the murder. We want to read on to find out what happens to him and what will the men do. He explains how 'one turned around' and shouted out in Zulu. This makes me tense as I only know Zulu as a war cry. This means I expect them to attack him, which is what they do. 'They began to run towards me… if they caught me I would follow their victim into the gallery'. This builds tension as he's running for his life. We want to read on to see what happens.

answer 4

Obed claims that he 'would have stayed in the mines' if he had not witnessed 'a terrible thing'. This makes us puzzled, wondering how terrible this 'thing' must be to turn Obed out of a job which provided him with good money. It also makes us apprehensive as it is very ominous but it is not clear what happened. Obed goes on to describe how he had been working for 'fifteen years' and he had a 'much better job' as an assistant to a blaster which tells us that he was happy with his work, again making us wonder what could have caused him to leave. However the mention of 'explosives' leads us to wonder if it has anything to do with it. When he is walking down the tunnel to fetch the 'sandwich tin', the description makes us uneasy and we sense danger. It was dimly lit but great care was required as there were 'great galleries' blasted out

Reading Units

of the rock which it was easy to fall down. The galleries could be up to 200ft deep'. This conveys to the reader Obed's precarious position and the potential danger he is in if he does not take care. As he turns a corner, which makes us jump as whatever is round the corner is not going to be good, the 'warning sign' confirms our worries, making us feel nervous. He sees four men holding a man 'by his arms and legs'. They are very much in control and they throw him 'over the edge and into the dark'. This shocks the reader and we are upset for the man. The man 'screamed something about a child' and it pulls at our heart strings to think that the man is being murdered, leaving what we assume is his child, fatherless. 'He was gone' is all very definite. When the men turn on Obed and shout in Zulu we feel panic. Obed is certain that if he is caught he will follow the man into the gallery'. The reader also knows this and we are desperate for Obed to get away. The sentence 'it was not a race I could let myself lose' shows Obed's desperate situation and panic to get away from the danger. He is racing for his life. The situation is very tense and because we are constantly informed of Obed's feelings, the reader gets involved with the dramatic situation.

- Answer 1 is the least successful because there is very little focus on the actual question. There is no mention of the murder and the chase so the coverage is very limited. There is no real engagement with the text and narrative technique. There are many vague assertions but there is no evidence or exploration. This would probably score 1 out of 10.
- Answer 2 would be placed next and is a classic example of what the students shouldn't write! It spots a couple of words but they are not put in any sort of context. This would probably score 2 out of 10.
- Answer 3 would be next as it makes some valid points and includes some relevant material. However the quality is a bit inconsistent as the references to 'rhythm' and 'short sentences' aren't relevant. This would score 6 out of 10.
- Answer 4 is the best. It remains closely on task throughout and tracks the text carefully and methodically. There is very good selection of material and the response is clear and coherent. It understands the narrative techniques. This would score 10 out of 10.

Unit 8
Comparing writers' ideas

LEARNING OBJECTIVES

▶ To identify the main themes and ideas in a text
▶ To interpret these ideas through critical reading
▶ To compare and evaluate these ideas across more than one text

This unit helps to prepare students for Section A of Component 2 of the written examination: 19th and 21st century non-fiction reading. The time allocation for this section is 1 hour, comprising 10 minutes' reading and 50 minutes' writing. It is worth 40 marks – 30% of the qualification.

Candidates are assessed on their understanding of two extracts (about 900–1200 words in total) of high-quality non-fiction writing, one from the 19th century, the other from the 21st century, assessed through a range of structured questions. This section assesses AO1, AO2, AO3 and AO4. The following unit deals with assessment objectives AO1 and AO3.

Assessment Objectives

AO1 ■ Identify and interpret explicit and implicit information and ideas.
AO3 ■ Compare writers' ideas and perspectives, as well as how these are conveyed, across two or more texts.

The aims of the unit should be made clear. The specification outlines that students should read a range of texts so that they can develop their understanding of different writers' ideas and the ways these are presented. This unit presents the skills needed for students to examine writers' similar or differing viewpoints.

Get going

Step 1 Work on your skills

ACTIVITY 1

The aim of this activity is to encourage students to begin to read **critically.**

Students read the three given extracts, identify the main idea of each one (what the writer appears to think about the subject) and find a quote which led them to form this opinion.

Answers

Topic	What does the writer appear to think about the topic?	Quote from the extract that led me to form this opinion
Motor neurone disease	It is a harsh condition.	'cruel'
Paris	Everyone in Paris is unfriendly.	'Why does everyone hate me so much?'
Biker, Danny Macaskill	Danny Macaskill is a skilled sportsperson.	'take on a death-defying ride'

Reading Units

ACTIVITY 2

Students should complete the fourth column with a brief analysis of the quote chosen for column 3. Students are now assessing **how** the writer conveys their ideas.

Answers

Topic	What does the writer appear to think about the topic?	Quote from the extract that lead me to form this opinion	Analysis
Motor neurone disease	It is a harsh condition.	'cruel'	The disease is personified, as if it actually wants to cause harm.
Paris	Everyone in Paris is unfriendly.	'Why does everyone hate me so much?'	'Everyone' is hyperbolic but shows the extent of the hostility. 'Hate' is a strong word.
Danny Macaskill	Danny Macaskill is a skilled sportsperson.	'take on a death-defying ride'	Compound adjective implies danger.

Extension Activity

Linked to the guidelines in the Top tips, students could develop their response to the three extracts by considering their own reaction to the topics.

Students should consider how the writer wishes the reader to react but should not include personal opinions that are not directly related to the text.

They can write up each row from the table to build a full answer, adding a final comment on the effect of the technique on the reader. The exercise encourages engagement with the writers' ideas.

For example:

> The writer illustrates that motor neurone disease is a harsh condition in the use of the word 'cruel.' The adjective personifies the disease, as if it actually wants to cause harm and conveys the symptoms of the condition as shocking.

Word bank
- Shocking
- Striking
- Surprising
- Impressive
- Upsetting

Step 2 Practise your skills

ACTIVITY 3

You may wish the students to read the extracts and attempt the questions themselves.

Alternatively, the tables provided below will lead less confident students through structuring their response.

Answers

Ideas about walking	Evidence from *A Walk in the Woods*	Evidence from *The Lady's Guide to Perfect Gentility*
People will not walk outdoors for even short distances.	'gets in her car to go a quarter of a mile.'	'from two to four miles would… appear to be an effort far too violent.'
People make excuses not to do it.	The gym provides 'a program' but nature is 'thoughtlessly deficient… in this regard.'	It is 'suited only to those as are compelled by necessity.'
People need to be persuaded to do it.	'I asked her once why she didn't walk to the gym and do five minutes less on the treadmill'	'two to four miles … is precisely such an amount of exercise as they stand most in need of.'

Go over the different question types given in the Student's Book, discussing what each question is asking students to do.

ACTIVITY 4

A fourth column has been added to the table. With attention to the writers' techniques, students should analyse how their ideas are conveyed.

Unit 8 Comparing writers' ideas

Answers

Ideas about walking	Evidence from *A Walk in the Woods*	Evidence from *The Lady's Guide to Perfect Gentility*	How the writers convey their ideas
People will not walk outdoors for even short distances.	'gets in her car to go a quarter of a mile.'	'from two to four miles would… appear to be an effort far too violent.'	Facts are used by both writers to convey that people will not even walk short distances. It appears that we have become lazier over time, as Thornwell cites 'two to four miles' as being regarded as too far by some people, but Bryson cites only 'a quarter of a mile' as too far.
People make excuses not to do it.	The gym provides 'a program' but nature is 'thoughtlessly deficient… in this regard.'	It is 'suited only to those as are compelled by necessity.'	The writers identify that people make excuses not to walk outdoors. Bryson knows a woman who drives to her nearby gym instead of walking because she likes to have 'a program' on the treadmill. The ridiculous situation of driving to a gym is mocked by Bryson, who comments sarcastically that it is 'thoughtlessly deficient' of nature not to provide a 'program' for outdoor walking. Thornwell is also critical and highlights lazy people who think that walking is only for those 'who are compelled by necessity' to walk and have no other option.
People need to be persuaded to do it.	'I asked her once why she didn't walk to the gym and do five minutes less on the treadmill'	'two to four miles … is precisely such an amount of exercise as they stand most in need of.'	Bryson suggests that the woman could walk to the gym and 'do five minutes less on the treadmill'. Similarly, Thornwell suggests that walking a few miles is 'precisely' what people are 'most in need of'.

Familiarise students with the key terms in the Top tips box that signpost that they are comparing or contrasting.

Step 3 Challenge yourself

ACTIVITY 5

This should be a full answer, structured as follows:

- technique used
- evidence from the text
- effect on the reader.

The Student's Book advises looking for the following techniques:

- negative language
- use of adjectives
- spoken comments
- a negative tone
- repetition
- use of fact and opinion.

You may wish to provide part of the table below for students who lack confidence.

Possible answers

Technique	Evidence from the *Mail Online*	Evidence from 'How to combine elegance, style and economy'	Effect
Negative language	'never been taught how to behave' 'lack a work ethic'	'the most hateful of all dispositions'	Young people are presented very unfavourably.
Use of adjectives	'sloppy' 'slovenly'	'haughty and overbearing'	Negative traits are identified.
Spoken comments	Sir Michael Wilshaw says 'they are not going to get a job'	Whole piece is opinion of the author – her comments.	Head of Ofsted and author of guide to manners give 'expert' observations.
Repetition	'dress inappropriately, speak inappropriately.'	Personal pronoun 'you' employed regularly.	Emphasises that more than one aspect of behaviour is 'inappropriate.' 'You' – direct address.
Fact and opinion	Whole piece is opinion of Sir Michael Wilshaw.	Thornwell's opinions are presented as facts. Imperatives reinforce this.	Opinions are stated as facts to lend confidence and force to the piece.

51

Reading Units

Improve your skills

LEARNING OBJECTIVES

▶ To read and evaluate texts critically
▶ To present informed judgements of the impact of different ideas in texts
▶ To summarise and synthesise information and ideas from two texts
▶ To connect, compare and contrast writers' techniques

Step 1 Work on your skills

ACTIVITY 1

Students will need a copy of the extracts on which they can add highlighting.

Students should identify evidence that conveys the writers' different experiences and begin to pick out the techniques that do this.

The Student's Book provides the following table of techniques that students may have identified. They can review what they have found.

	Extract 1	Extract 2
First person narrative	'I was then escorted'	'I refused to be held'
Use of positive or negative language	'I was pleasantly surprised'	'convulsive fear', 'agony'
Detail	Gown was like 'a circus tent.'	'the glitter of polished steel'
Sentence length	Both long and short. Very clear and straightforward.	Mostly long with subordinate clauses. Hyphens. Inter-sentential punctuation.
Use of verbs	'inserted'	'plunged'
Use of adjectives	'high-tech'	'excruciating'
Tone	Cheerful. Jokey imagery. Exclamation marks.	Dramatic. Striking.

Then, discuss the differences between the two patients' accounts of the same medical procedure and the possible reasons for these differences. The following further discussion point is provided in the Student's Book:

- How could you tell that the first describes a modern operation and the second, 19th-century surgery?

Extension Activity

A fourth column can be drawn up, in which students analyse the differences between the effects of the writers' different language choices and techniques. Suggestions are shown below.

Technique	Extract 1	Extract 2	Effect
First person narrative	'I was then escorted'	'I refused to be held'	'escorted' – polite/relaxed 'refused', 'held' – restrictive
Use of positive or negative language	'I was pleasantly surprised'	'convulsive fear,' 'agony'	'pleasantly' – positive adverb 'fear', 'agony' – very frightening
Detail	Gown was like 'a circus tent.'	'the glitter of polished steel'	1 – jokey simile 2 – frightening visual imagery
Sentence length	Both long and short. Very clear and straight forward.	Mostly long with subordinate clauses. Hyphens. Inter-sentential punctuation.	1 – varied style 2 – long sentences draw out the agonies of the experience
Use of verbs	'inserted'	'plunged'	The second example is more dramatic/violent.
Use of adjectives	'high-tech'	'excruciating'	1 – reassuring 2 – horribly painful
Tone	Cheerful. Jokey imagery. Exclamation marks.	Dramatic. Striking.	Striking differences between the patients' experiences

You may wish to set an additional task for students to write up their answer in full.

The Top tips box on page 92 provides additional guidance on the structure of comparative responses.

Unit 8 Comparing writers' ideas

Step 2 Practise your skills

ACTIVITY 2

The Student's Book suggests that the students may wish to consider the use of:

- hyperbolic language
- verbs (the most notable are identified)
- adjectives
- modal verbs (defined in the Student's Book)
- a formal or informal tone.

Hyperbolic language	Use of verbs	Use of adjectives	Use of a modal verb	Formal or informal tone
Extract 1				
He made me believe in magic	comparing		can	informal tone
He was a genius	gabbles	bankrupt		
	claims			
Extract 2				
take its rightful place in the foremost rank of English Elegiac Verse	confess	ignorant	should	formal tone
be known and loved by thousands of thoughtful and appreciative readers	received	rightful	will	
	indulge	foremost		
	known	thoughtful		
	live	appreciative		
	loved			

Organising your answer

A framework for connecting texts is provided in the Student's Book. It is completed with a sample answer in the example below. Students can be provided with this as an example to start their own response.

Question: What are the writers' opinions of the abilities of the people they are writing about? How do they convey these opinions? Can you make any connections, comparisons or contrasts between the writers' ideas and techniques?		
Text 1: 'Genius or Hype?'	Conversely,...	Text 2: Response to Shelley's 'Adonaïs'
Point that I'm trying to make: Hart is highly critical of Michael Jackson, saying that nothing he created can compare with the talent of...		Point that I'm trying to make: Wise claims that the person he is writing about, Shelley, is extremely talented but not everyone recognises this.
Evidence: 'Shakespeare and Michaelangelo'. Key words to help in my explanation: Hart mocks people's definition of Jackson as a 'genius' and, instead, gives examples of those he believes are worthy of this term.		Evidence: He says that these people's reaction is 'ignorant'... Key words to help in my explanation: because Shelley's work should be 'loved'.

53

Reading Units

Step 3 Challenge yourself

ACTIVITY 3

Extract 1: The painful truth about trainers: Are running shoes a waste of money?

Answers

1. What is the main idea of this newspaper piece? Running barefoot is better than wearing expensive running shoes.
2. How does the writer convince you that he knows his subject? He'd 'spent years' running in unsuitable shoes so knows his subject.
3. From what perspective is he writing? Subjective – he has experience of this problem.
4. What conclusion is reached about specialist running shoes? Expensive running shoes are a waste of money.

Extract 2: Attire for the female cyclist – 1895

Answers

1. What is the main idea of this newspaper piece? That women need advice as to what to wear when riding a bicycle.
2. From what perspective is the journalist writing? Ostensibly, it is objective – the writer would probably claim that this is an advisory piece. However, the writer holds strong opinions and is not impartial so we could regard it as a subjective piece.

Students should be reminded to use the P-E-E structure:

- **P**oint – **E**vidence – **E**xplanation

When comparing and contrasting texts, this can take the form of:

- **P**oint – **E**vidence from Text 1 – **E**vidence from Text 2 – **E**xplanation

As students are now familiar with the texts, allow them about 12 minutes to answer this question.

Students can use the table in the Student's Book to mark their own or a peer's response.

Extension Activity

Students can also use the same self-assessment table to mark the following response out of 10.

> The effect of these two pieces is closely bound up with the language and perspective that they both use. Extract 1 poses the question, 'Are running shoes a waste of money?' This approach involves the reader and suggests the writer's impartiality. He begins in third person narrative, then reports a dialogue between two people that are experts. The coach is 'well-respected' and claims his runners 'run faster' barefoot. He sounds knowledgeable so we trust his judgement. The writer ends with his own first person narrative experience of running shoes, and says the coach's claims come as 'no surprise.' He then uses a conclusion from a doctor that borders on being a punchline, in 'buy a bike.' This blend of personal experience and expert testimony is convincing and makes the sales representatives look foolish – something we all enjoy.

> The second extract appears to be giving impartial advice to female cyclists but its commanding tone in 'there are words of wisdom to be followed', use of imperatives in the repetition of 'Don't' and concentration on what should not be worn, make it a negative piece of work. It is a more serious piece than extract 1. The second writer takes on the role as 'expert.' However, phrases such as 'women... of high or low degree' demonstrate that this is a judgemental piece from someone who believes they know more than those they are writing about. Conversely, the writer of the first piece agrees with the coach and has his own experience of this subject. The first writer ends with the jokey advice, 'buy a bike' but the second extract ends with the patronising advice, 'There is no need for every item of your attire to match' and we feel a dislike for this anonymous writer.

This answer would receive full marks.

BE EXAM READY

LEARNING OBJECTIVES

▶ To interpret writers' ideas
▶ To synthesise these ideas
▶ To analyse writers' techniques and connect, compare and contrast them

Introduction

The aim of this section is to combine the skills students have built up in this unit in analysis of the text below.

Question 1

Including a reading of the texts, allow about 20 minutes to answer this question.

The P-E-E structure should be provided:

- **P**oint – **E**xample – **E**xplanation

Suggested word banks were given in Unit 3 of the Teacher's Book (see page 16).

You may wish students to structure their answers using the table provided in the Student's Book, or you may choose to provide further guidance from the completed table below in order to differentiate support between students (see Dynamic Learning).

A fourth column of effects has also been added for your guidance.

Techniques	Extract 1	Extract 2	Effect
Title	'Morning Strength Training'	'Silver Sprinters: defying-age athletes'	1 – clear and instructive 2 – sibilance. 'Defying-age' compound adjective.
Main ideas	Men's easy exercises	Exercise can be done at any age.	Extract 2 is more inclusive.
Grammar	Mostly long, complex sentences	Varied sentence length and some sentence fragments, 'Just good stuff.'	1 – suitable for describing detail of exercises 2 – variety adds interest
Structure	List of logical instructions: 'On rising', 'Then', 'After', 'Next', 'Finally'	Examples, guidelines, expert advice	Both are clear. Extract 2 is more varied in its content.
Language choices	Not too much jargon. Verbs: 'curl', 'lift', 'hold' 'Duty', 'work' – suggests obligation Adjectives: 'vigorous', 'best-known', 'ample', 'splendid' – denote effective exercises Adverbs: 'rapidly' and 'continuously' – how to do the exercises 'loins' – archaic word	Some technical vocabulary: 'heart rate', 'oxygen', 'body fat', 'reduced capacity' Advisory tone: 'But', 'However', 'just remember' Noun: 'chore' Verbs: 'plays', 'eats', 'takes' – lively tone Adjective: 'defying-age athletes' Informal language: 'young at heart', 'fitness kick'	1 – aimed at male fitness enthusiasts. Instructive 2 – aimed at a wide audience. Lively and engaging
Facts	'fifteen minutes,' 'a hundred times.'	'age 72,' 'in his 70s,' '40 marathons.'	1 – clearly instructive 2 – emphasis on age and amount of sport
Expert advice	Blaikie is a fitness 'enthusiast.'	Case studies. NHS guidelines. Sports physician.	Blaikie has more of a personal interest in his subject.

Reading Units

Techniques	Extract 1	Extract 2	Effect
Personal pronouns	Male pronoun 'let him' seems unusual to a modern reader.	Pronouns are used but there is an emphasis on names.	1 – dictates that the exercises are only for men. Instructive 2 – piece relies on interviewees
Dramatic punctuation	Lots of inter-sentential punctuation.	Questions.	1 – delineates instructions 2 – interrogative mood involves the reader

Self-assessment

Students may wish to mark their own work or peer-assess a work partner's response.

A self-assessment guide of possible points is included in the Student's Book.

Sample answers

Answers and examiner's commentaries are provided in the Student's Book.

The first response has been awarded 5 marks. The second response has been awarded 8 marks.

Students could continue these answers so that both score 10 marks.

Unit 9
Comparing language

LEARNING OBJECTIVES

▶ To read texts with awareness of the writer's use of language and techniques
▶ To compare the techniques used in more than one text
▶ To evaluate writers' techniques from more than one text

This unit helps to prepare students for Section A of Component 2 of the written examination: 19th and 21st century non-fiction reading. The time allocation for this section is 1 hour, comprising 10 minutes' reading and 50 minutes' writing. It is worth 40 marks – 30% of the qualification.

Candidates are assessed on their understanding of two extracts (about 900–1200 words in total) of high-quality non-fiction writing, one from the 19th century, the other from the 21st century, assessed through a range of structured questions.

Assessment Objectives

AO1 ▪ Identify and interpret explicit and implicit information and ideas.
AO2 ▪ Explain, comment on and analyse how writers use language and structure to achieve effects and influence readers, using relevant subject terminology to support their views
AO3 ▪ Compare writers' ideas and perspectives, as well as how these are conveyed, across two or more texts.
AO4 ▪ Evaluate texts critically and support this with appropriate textual references.

The aims of the unit should be made clear. The specification outlines that students should read critically, evaluating writers' vocabulary choices and comparing how writers do this in different texts, using linguistic and literary terminology accurately.

Get going

Step 1 Work on your skills

ACTIVITY 1

The aim of this activity is to evaluate writers' vocabulary choices.

The key terms remind students of the main parts of speech. They should read over this to familiarise themselves with these.

Extension Activity

In preparation for identifying the techniques used in the two letters, put the following words on the board. Ask students to identify the nouns, adjectives, verbs and adverbs.

- Nouns: parents, holiday
- Adjectives: smug, rubbish, irritating
- Verbs: invited, approved, tell
- Adverbs: absolutely, scarcely

Ask students to feed back their answers.

57

Reading Units

Technique	Letter 1 example	Effect	Letter 2 example	Effect
Narrative stance	First person narrative	Outlines a personal problem	First person narrative	Makes the invitation sincere
Structure of the extract	States problem. Gives opinion of family members. Appeals for advice	The nature of the writer's problem is made clear.	Writer states opinion of friend and invites them to stay.	Flatters friend in the hope they'll accept the subsequent invitation
Mood	'depressing me enormously'	Invites our sympathy	'be a real enjoyment to me'	An uplifting mood
Positive language	'They're lovely'	Compliments the parents but aim is probably to emphasise that she is a reasonable person	'pleasure in your society'	Compliments her friend and emphasises the joy that her company brings
Negative language	'absolutely rubbish'	The writer seems determined not to enjoy her holiday.	'am selfish enough'	This is used in an unusual way. The writer wants the friend's company and acknowledges that this may seem 'selfish'
Personal feelings	'I can't stand the thought'	Has spent a lot of time thinking about this problem	Could re-use any examples in previous three boxes	The writer is very fond of the friend's company
Adjectives (describing words)	Mostly negative: 'smug', 'painful', 'rubbish', 'irritating', 'serious'	Makes clear how unhappy the writer is about their situation	'dear', 'great', 'sincere', 'humble' and 'rural retreat'	Writer compliments their friend and is modest about their home in comparison to New York
Verbs (action words)	'invited', 'don't want', 'never really approved', 'can't stand'	Outlines the letter's main issue. Most other verbs are negative	'tell', 'feel', 'covet', 'leave', 'making', 'enliven'	Makes the writer's purpose clear and conveys their hopes
Adverbs (tell us more about how an action is done or the extent of someone's feelings)	'depressing me enormously' 'absolutely rubbish'	Makes feelings of sadness clear	'I need scarcely tell you.'	Makes friendship clear
Abstract nouns (feelings and qualities)	'no patience'	Emphasises feelings	'pleasure', 'enjoyment'	Positive feelings

ACTIVITY 2

Language techniques from each text have been identified in the table provided above. Students fill in the blank boxes, commenting on the effects they think the techniques create.

Students should familiarise themselves with the useful phrases for cross-referencing texts in the Top tips box.

Step 2 | Practise your skills

ACTIVITY 3

Having completed the exercises in Work on your skills, students should now have the skills to answer a full question on the letters they have studied.

On completion of their answer, students can use the table completed in Activity 2 to assess their or a peer's work. They could also follow the annotated examples in the student's answer to annotate a peer's response.

Step 3 | Challenge yourself

ACTIVITY 4

Students will need a copy of the texts on which they can add highlighting. This activity could be undertaken independently or in pairs.

This should be a full answer, structured as follows:
- Technique used
- Evidence from the text
- Effect on the reader

58

Unit 9 Comparing language

When comparing and contrasting texts, this can take the form of:
- **P**oint – **E**vidence from Text 1 – **E**vidence from Text 2 – **E**xplanation

Including reading time, allow about 15 minutes to answer the question.

The Student's Book advises looking for the following techniques:
- narrative stance
- the structure of the extracts
- mood
- sentence structures
- conjunctions to start sentences
- positive language
- adjectives
- verbs
- adverbs
- abstract nouns

A detailed self-assessment section, covering the techniques listed above, is included in the Student's Book.

You may wish to give students a copy of the following example to mark.

> Both extracts are in third person narrative to show that the writers are observers. Ideas of times are given in both, in 'ten minutes later' and 'the morning'. This gives the reader a sense of being there too. There is a sense of amazement in both, shown in 'collective gasp' and 'could not damp the joy'. There are different length sentences to keep our interest. There are lots of positive words in both, such as, 'great unveiling', 'timeless triumph' and 'magnificence'.

Examiner's commentary

This is an accurate answer which does not quite fulfil its potential. Third person narrative is identified and the effect is explained briefly. The point about time is well organised and explained. Quotes to prove a sense of amazement are well chosen but not explained. The effect of using different sentence lengths is touched on but no examples are given for support. Positive word selections are well chosen but the effect of these is not explained.

This answer scores 5.

Improve your skills

LEARNING OBJECTIVES

▶ To analyse writers' subject specific vocabulary
▶ To offer judgements about writers' language choices for their intended audience
▶ To compare and evaluate writers' techniques

This section of the unit concentrates on developing students' attention to writers' specific language choices and comparing how different writers use these techniques.

Step 1 Work on your skills

ACTIVITY 1

Students read the extracts and complete the table with a list of subject specific words that the writer uses. Some examples are provided.

Suggested answers

Subject: Board games	
Subject specific words in Extract 1	Subject specific words in Extract 2
player	edition
move	popular
pawns	game
track	questions
spaces	pace
piece	play
advance	teams
go back	answer
return	wedge
Intended audience: Suggestions are included in the Student's Book.	

59

Reading Units

ACTIVITY 2

With a work partner, students should discuss any points of comparison between the language used.

This discussion effectively forms the start of the answer to the question:

Compare how the writers convey their ideas about smoking.

Suggested answers are given in the Student's Book.

ACTIVITY 3

The beginning of an exemplar answer is supplied to the following question:

Compare how the writers convey their ideas about smoking.

Using the ideas discussed in the activities above, students should continue the response.

This should be a full answer, structured as follows:

- **P**oint – **E**xample from Text 1 – **E**xample from Text 2 – **E**xplanation

As students are already familiar with the text, allow about 12 minutes to answer the question.

The vocabulary list in the Activity 2 table and the Student's Book notes on intended audience serve as an effective self-assessment guide. Students can also add examiner's annotations to their own or peer's responses.

Draw students' attention to the ten phrases to avoid and how to improve them in the Top tips box.

Step 2 Practise your skills

ACTIVITY 4

Suggestions of features of the two extracts are given below:

- The word 'nature' in the first extract is at odds with the idea of 'unwritten rules' in the second piece. The first extract suggests that dancing comes naturally to people. By contrast, the second implies that certain rules need to be followed.
- Both writers come to conclusions about dancing by being observers. Extract 1's third person narrator is an observer. It says that dancers who 'might be seen' without the music being heard are a 'strange' sight. In visualising this, we become more involved in the piece. The second writer uses first person narrative to relate their personal experiences to us in the phrase, 'I've noticed.' This suggests that their judgement may be trusted.
- The language choices also convey which extract is modern and which is from the 19th century. Nouns such as 'blendings' and 'invocation' are seldom used today but would be easily comprehensible to a 19th-century reader. Similarly, the second extract uses words such as 'mosh pit' and 'gig' which suggests that the writer has particular genre 'fans' in mind, in this case, fans of 'punk and metal' shows. Each writer uses language suitable for their intended audience.

Draw students' attention to the first writer's use of third person narrative and the second writer's use of first person narrative.

Extension Activity 1

The table below contains quotes from the extract 'Ten rules of mosh pit etiquette'.

Give students a copy of the table with only the first column completed (which can be found on Dynamic Learning).

Students complete the second column by identifying the effect of the first person narrative.

Evidence	Effect
'In my years attending punk and metal shows,'	The writer has spent time researching their subject.
'I've noticed…'	The writer is observant.
'wait for the slower, heavier sections'	Direct address
'if you're not prepared'	Conversational style
'try to pace yourself'	Advises the reader from the point of view of someone who has experience.

Extension Activity 2

In writing about the effect of writers' language choices, students can be more exacting in their analysis by using precise vocabulary themselves.

Students who describe attitudes or effects as **positive** or **negative** should only use this term once. Explaining how this impression is created and using

Unit 9 Comparing language

other adjectives to replace positive and negative, such as 'an optimistic attitude' or 'a critical approach' will make students' answers more analytical.

Ask students to list as many alternatives for positive and negative as possible. Some suggestions are provided here.

Alternative for positive	Alternative for negative
supportive	dismissive
favourable	unfavourable
affirmative	disdainful
approving	critical
complimentary	derogatory
uplifting	reproachful
reassuring	discouraging
optimistic	disparaging

Step 3 Challenge yourself

ACTIVITY 5

Language techniques from each text have been identified in the table in the Student's Book. Students complete the blank boxes, commenting on the effects of the techniques.

You may wish students to write this up as a full answer. The completed table can then be given as a guide to peer-/self-assessment.

Technique	Examples in Extract 1	Examples in Extract 2	Effect of technique
Subject specific words	'coffee', 'beverage', 'cup', 'sipping'	'coffee', 'Starbucks', 'powder', 'jar', 'flat white', 'cup', 'shot of espresso', 'beverages', 'outlets'	Indicates the subject matter clearly
Possible intended audience	Text is a 'History [of] Producing Coffee'	'How much would you pay…?'	Extract 1 – those with a particular interest in the subject Extract 2 – wider audience
Narrative stance	Third person narrative	Subtle use of first person narrative in the phrase, 'For most of us'	Extract 1 – factual, historical account Extract 2 – subtly includes us to engage the reader
Positive language	'fashion', 'fashionable', 'treated', 'personage', 'impress' (Note that 'extravagant' is used negatively to describe a high price.)	'willing', 'reasonable', 'no problem'	Extract 1 – coffee is presented as a luxury Extract 2 – coffee is presented as relatively affordable
Negative language	'beyond affordability', 'extravagant price', 'confined'	'paying in excess'	Extract 1 – presented as out of reach for the 'common man' Extract 2 – we are willing to pay more for a luxury coffee
Any other interesting use of words	'Turkish ambassador', 'servant'	'psychological barrier'	Extract 1 – rich, upper-classes Extract 2 – we adjust easily to rising prices

BE EXAM READY

LEARNING OBJECTIVES

▶ To analyse a writer's use of language and techniques
▶ To compare and evaluate writers' techniques
▶ To put these skills into practice in a timed question

Begin by recapping on the skills acquired in this unit:

- Reading texts with an understanding of the writer's language and techniques
- Comparing and evaluating these techniques across different texts

The aim of this section is to combine these skills in analysis of the following texts.

Question 1

Students will need a copy of the extracts on which they can add highlighting.

Students should read the extracts about extreme endeavours and then answer the question.

The comparing and contrasting of the texts should be structured as follows:

- **P**oint – **E**vidence from Text 1 – **E**vidence from text 2 – **E**xplanation

Including reading time, allow about 15 minutes to answer the question.

Students can use the self–assessment section in the Student's Book to mark their answer.

Next, students should read sample answers 1 and 2 in the Student's Book, annotate these with comments and decide on a mark for each answer.

Suggested examiner's commentaries are supplied for distribution to students after completion of this exercise.

Examiner's commentary on sample answer 1

The candidate engages with the question and shows awareness of how the writers makes the feats sound dangerous. Selections from the text are usually well chosen and are quite precise. Arguably, the first point about dying is a little repetitive. There is a slight misreading in stating that Blondin's heart is 'fluttering' as this describes the crowd more than him. Precise textual reference is selected in the second part of the passage. Selections could be analysed in more depth. The answer could be extended but scores 6 as it is.

Examiner's commentary on sample answer 2

This is a thoughtful answer that explores a nice variety of the writers' techniques. The candidate makes a confident start and supports points appropriately. There is careful selection of textual reference, shown in gathering together all the references to death in the first extract and finding a comparative quote in 'perdition' from the second.

Comparison of the writers' language is shown again in selecting quotes which illustrate feelings of nervousness.

The narrative approach is tackled confidently.

The candidate explores how tension is created and embeds quotation nicely. Well-chosen adjectives are commented on. To develop the answer even further, these could be analysed in a little more depth, but serve to support the considered point that the reader feels as if 'they are watching'. The response scores 9.

Unit 10
Using textual references

LEARNING OBJECTIVES

▶ To be able to differentiate between different types of textual references
▶ To be precise in the use of textual references

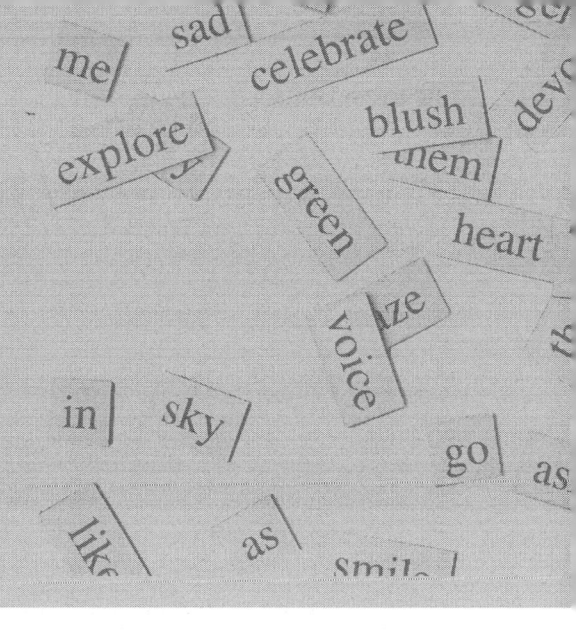

Assessment Objectives

AO4 ■ Evaluate texts critically and support this with appropriate textual references

Get going

Step 1 | Work on your skills

ACTIVITY 1

To support the first activity, give students a copy of the text. Get them to block out words and sentences until they are left with a focus on the basic events.

They can then complete the student activity. Valid discussions can be had around different decisions and choices made by the students. In the first few lines, students might block out the following words:

- They began in Westminster and the wailing moan rippled outwards to the suburbs.
- as he had learnt to do in the army.

Step 2 | Practise your skills

ACTIVITY 2

Answers to the Wasteland activity could include:

- He escapes into a wilderness of old cars and scrap.
- Something catches him by the leg and he brings his stick down on top of it.
- He pushes on but his followers keep up with him.
- The barbed wire tears at him.
- He cries out.
- He escapes and he sees a bus approaching and a man close by.

Make sure students make at least five textual references, and support them with quotations.

Step 3 | Challenge yourself

ACTIVITY 3

Draw students' attention to the key terms 'explicit information' and 'implicit information' on page 123 in the Student's Book before beginning this activity.

Answers

Textual reference	Inference
'[Dad] always kept his promises'	The main character has faith in his father.
'I was in the team for the big one'	This is a big day for the narrator.
'He'd never missed a game.'	The father has previously been dedicated to supporting his son.
'I kept looking beyond the pitch'	The narrator is distracted by the fact that his father is not there.
'I was gutted.'	The narrator feels very let down and emotional.
'It was all her fault.'	The narrator blames someone else, a female, not his father.
'Still, he'd come in the end. I knew Dad.'	The narrator still has a strong belief or faith in his father.

63

Reading Units

ACTIVITY 4

Students should complete the table as shown below and then write their paragraph.

Textual reference	Inference
Animals are 'rescued'.	People at the Shamwari reserve are kind.
The 'dirt road at the entrance'.	The environment is quite undeveloped.
An 'animal I'd never seen before'.	The writer is from a different environment.

Improve your skills

LEARNING OBJECTIVES

- To further develop the ability to differentiate between different types of textual references
- To consider textual references in terms of vocabulary and writers' techniques
- To consider textual references in terms of gaining an overview of a text

Step 1 | Work on your skills

ACTIVITY 1

An interesting way into this activity is to begin by giving the words below to students (they are the answers to the student activity).

dark	shivered	silence
strange	terrified	hostile
stumbled	cackle	vanished
dim	low	animal-like
greasily	sickened	flared
stuffy	bewildered	

As a class, discuss the overall effect of these words. Ask students to make predictions as to what the text might be about. Then ask them to add three or four words to the list that would not look out of place.

Discuss how these words might be used in a descriptive piece of text and what the overall effect would be. Students could diamond rank the words in terms of effectiveness or organise them into groups.

After this, they could complete the activity in the Student's Book.

Step 2 | Practise your skills

ACTIVITY 2

Activity 1 goes hand in hand with this writing activity – students need a clear focus on key words.

The following are suggestions of words the students may come up with:

> The bus filled quickly with a <u>surge</u> of people, <u>cloying</u> and <u>clamouring</u> for a seat. It was soon <u>packed</u> with people. Those <u>fortunate</u> individuals who had managed a coveted chair were not to be easily shifted! Many of them looked <u>impassively</u> ahead, as if willing the crowd around away. One man – smug in his <u>window-seated</u> comfort – had the trace of a <u>slyly</u> satisfied smile on his face.

Step 3 | Challenge yourself

ACTIVITY 3

Test students' understanding by asking them to match the definition with the technique. Display or give students a version of the table below on which the definitions are not lined up (which can be found on Dynamic Learning).

Associated imagery	Makes you think of something else (often as a simile or metaphor)
Alliteration	Repeated sounds
Plosive	A consonant that is produced by stopping the airflow followed by a sudden release of air (for example, b, p)
Complex sentence	Extra information in a sentence
Action verb	Gives a sense of movement
Onomatopoeia	Sound words
Speech	Reported words spoken by a person or character

With a good understanding of the terms, students can now complete a table with examples from the text and explanations of the effects of the techniques (which is

Unit 10 Using textual references

provided on Dynamic Learning). A completed version is provided below.

Technique	Example from text	Explanation of effect
Associated imagery	'red forked lightning'	Links to the Devil – makes the weather fearful
Alliteration	'by practising all possible manoeuvres, to preserve the ship'	Gives impact to the ship's dangerous situation
Plosives	'burst… from the bosom of the big black clouds'	The plosive sounds reflect the noise of the storm.
Complex sentence	The last sentence of the passage	A sense of the amount of danger they are in is presented by a packed, building crescendo.
Action verbs	'pushed', 'driven', etc.	These words give a sense of the power and strength of the wind.
Onomatopoeia	'crash'	Gives a sense of the danger and noise of the storm
Speech	'none of us will see the morning.'	The doom-laden speech from an experienced seaman makes us fear the worst!

Extension Activity

Ask students to think about what each technique might add to the reading of a text (for example, plosives may create a forceful, angry mood).

ACTIVITY 4

To begin thinking about tone, you could begin by asking the students to alter each of these headlines as indicated:

Man, 25, marries woman, 88

Change from a factual tone to a humorous tone.

Thugs desecrate war memorial

Change from an angry tone to a more factual tone. Then change it to a more emotive tone.

Clown trips up in circus mishap!

Change from a light-hearted, humorous tone to a more serious tone.

Schoolboy admits crime

Change from a factual tone to an angrier tone.

The following are examples of extracts that could be chosen from the Bill Bryson extract to highlight how it is amusing.

Reference	Humorous because…
The shelter was 'as good as I was going to get'	It is not very good at all!
'It was all most fetching'	This is quite sarcastic – he is in no mood to appreciate the view!
'I used some woollen socks as mittens and put a pair of flannel boxer shorts on my head'	He is forced to look ridiculous and use his underwear as gloves and a hat!
'waited patiently for death's sweet kiss'	He wants to die, he is so cold and desperate!
Description of the dog	The owner is not giving the dog time to pee (maybe because it's so cold).
'"Transport calf?" I repeated uncertainly'	As an American, he has trouble understanding the man.
'removed the forgotten boxer shorts with a blush'	He has forgotten he has his underpants on his head!

ACTIVITY 5

As a way of thinking about this activity, students could consider the following and ask themselves if the answers are to be found in the text itself or 'outside' the text.

They should work with a learning partner to consider each of the following headings and place them in the table like the one the next page (an incomplete version of which is available on Dynamic Learning), depending on whether they can find them in the text or outside.

There may be discussion as to where they best fit and they may not neatly divide up into each section of the table.

- A statement by the writer, backed up with evidence
- A statement by the writer, not backed with relevant evidence
- The views and attitudes of the time the text was written

65

Reading Units

- Biases held by you about the topic
- Biases held by the writer about the topic
- Your own thoughts and feelings
- The views and attitudes of society today
- Knowledge of other texts/references of the time

	In the text	Outside the text
Decided by the writer	A statement by the writer, backed up with evidence A statement by the writer, not backed up with relevant evidence	Biases held by the writer about the topic
Decided by you		Biases held by you about the topic Your own thoughts and feelings Knowledge of other texts/references of the time
Decided by others		The views and attitudes of the time the text was written The views and attitudes of society today

ACTIVITY 6

Extract	Category and reason for the match
The use of the onomatopoeic word 'howling' makes the storm seem alive. It not only gives me a sense of the noise the wind was making, but gives me the idea that the storm was like an animal, preparing to attack.	Technique Discussion of onomatopoeia suggests that the student is discussing the writer's techniques.
Bill Bryson has a very uncomfortable night in a shelter on the sea front. This is clear through the bolts making comfort an 'impossibility'. This makes it clear that he is in for a hard, uncomfortable night.	Language The student discusses individual words.
It appears that the man is used to meeting all sorts of people. This impression is created because he carries on talking about the weather and doesn't seem bothered by the underpants on Bryson's head.	Inference The suggestion that the man meets lots of people has been worked out from his reaction to the unusual situation.
It is obvious that ordinary black families were very poor. The passage states that a single lamp 'lights one large room'. This gives a sense of the poverty at the time.	Overview This discusses wider issues of the time that the text throws up. This implies a sense of overview.
A sense of danger is built up through a series of happenings in the narrative – first Mike spots his attackers, then he runs into the wasteland. When he gets here, however, there are a series of other difficulties that he has to face.	Events The student picks out what happens (the events) in the passage.
The article is factual and informative. This is built up through a series of personal observations and facts about the reserve.	Tone The student is discussing an impression of the tone of the writing through the purpose.

BE EXAM READY

LEARNING OBJECTIVES

▶ To practise using a full range of textual references in an exam context
▶ To feel confident about writing under timed conditions

Question 1

This question tests the ability to evaluate texts critically and support this with appropriate textual references. The following mark scheme will enable you to review your answer.

0 marks	Give to responses where there is nothing worthy of credit.
1–2 marks	Give to responses that express a simple personal opinion with linked basic textual reference but struggle to engage with the text and/or the question, for example, I think the text shows what it is like to be on a boat in a storm.
3–4 marks	Give to responses that give a personal opinion supported by straightforward textual references. These responses will show limited interaction with the text, for example, I thought the text was exciting, wondering if Pi would survive.
5–6 marks	Give to responses that give an evaluation of the text and its effects, supported by appropriate textual references, for example, I think the writer builds the tension through language choices such as 'monstrous' to describe the unknown sounds being made as the ship is sinking.
7–8 marks	Give to responses that give a critical evaluation of the text's effects, supported by well-selected textual references. These responses will show clear engagement, for example, the writer builds suspense through a series of questions being used, which adds to the confused atmosphere.
9–10 marks	Give to responses that give a persuasive evaluation of the text and its effects, supported by convincing, well-selected examples and purposeful textual references. These responses will show engagement and involvement, where candidates take an overview to make accurate and perceptive comments, for example, Martell makes us feel sorry for Pi as he is treated quite roughly by the crewmembers. They speak different languages, which adds to the confusion.

Areas for evaluation:

- The situation – a boy alone on a sinking ship
- Inferences that the boy is scared, such as his babbling to the crew members
- The vocabulary used to build tension and confusion – adjectives such as 'monstrous' and verbs such as 'ran'
- Techniques such as a series of questions being used
- A wry humour – 'Only when they threw me overboard did I have doubts'
- Clear overview – the clash of ages/authority/culture between the boy and the crewmembers; the dire situation and its seriousness

Examiners are not looking for all these answers; they are merely suggestions. Any valid alternative answers not on this list will also gain credit. Refer to the mark boundaries to gauge the student's level of response.

Extension Activity

Read the following text carefully. It is a piece of travel writing about Pompeii, a town in Italy that was destroyed, but preserved, by a volcanic explosion in AD 79.

> In one of these long halls the skeleton of a man was found, with ten pieces of gold in one hand and a large key in the other. He had seized his money and started toward the door, but the fiery tempest caught him at the very threshold, and he sank down and died. One more minute of precious time would have saved him. I saw the skeletons of a man, a woman, and two young girls. The woman had her hands spread wide apart, as if in mortal terror, and I imagined I could still trace upon her shapeless face something of the expression of wild despair that distorted it when the heavens rained fire in these streets, so many ages ago. The girls and the man lay with their faces upon their arms, as if they had tried to shield them from the enveloping cinders.

67

Reading Units

> In one apartment eighteen skeletons were found, all in sitting postures, and blackened places on the walls still mark their shapes and show their attitudes, like shadows. One of them, a woman, still wore upon her skeleton throat a necklace, with her name engraved upon it – JULIE DI DIOMEDE.
>
> But perhaps the most poetical thing Pompeii has yielded to modern research, was that grand figure of a Roman soldier, clad in complete armor; who, true to his duty, true to his proud name of a soldier of Rome, and full of the stern courage which had given to that name its glory, stood to his post by the city gate, erect and unflinching, till the hell that raged around him burned out the dauntless spirit it could not conquer.
>
> We never read of Pompeii but we think of that soldier; we can not write of Pompeii without the natural impulse to grant to him the mention he so well deserves. Let us remember that he was a soldier – not a policeman – and so, praise him. Being a soldier, he stayed – because the warrior instinct forbade him to fly. Had he been a policeman he would have stayed, also – because he would have been asleep.
>
> *The Innocents Abroad* by Mark Twain, 1869

What are your thoughts and feelings as you read this text?

You should comment on:

- what is said
- how it is said.

You must refer to the text to support your comments

This question tests the ability to evaluate texts critically and support this with appropriate textual references.

0 marks	For responses where there is nothing worthy of credit.
1–2 marks	Give to responses that express a simple personal opinion with linked basic textual reference but struggle to engage with the text and/or the question, for example, I think the text makes me think of what it was like to be in Pompeii.
3–4 marks	Give to responses that give a personal opinion supported by straightforward textual references. These responses will show limited interaction with the text, for example, I thought the text was sad, as the man nearly survived but got caught.
5–6 marks	Give to responses that give an evaluation of the text and its effects, supported by appropriate textual references, for example, I think the writer builds the horror for the people who died in Pompeii, through language choices such as 'mortal terror' and 'wild despair'.
7–8 marks	Give to responses that give a critical evaluation of the text's effects, supported by well-selected textual references. They will show clear engagement, for example, the writer shows a respect to the people of Rome by a series of adjectives: 'proud', 'unflinching' and 'dauntless'.
9–10 marks	Give to responses that give a persuasive evaluation of the text and its effects, supported by convincing, well-selected examples and purposeful textual references. These responses will show engagement and involvement, where candidates take an overview to make accurate and perceptive comments, for example, Twain undercuts the serious tone of respect for the dead with a comparison of the soldier with a modern policeman. This is quite amusing.

Areas that students may explore:

- Details bring to life the reality of what it was like for the people, for example: 'ten pieces of gold in one hand and a large key in the other'.
- There is a sense of panic: 'seized his money'/'mortal terror'.
- The horror of what happened and the scale of disaster: 'fiery tempest'/'the heavens rained fire'.
- Frustration that 'One more minute of precious time would have saved him.'
- Written from a first person perspective: 'I saw…'/'I imagined…' makes it more immediate and allows us to consider the lives of the people who died.
- Sad reminder of a family: 'a man, a woman, and two young girls'.

- Number of people who died is emphasised: 'eighteen skeletons were found'.
- Sense of normality 'all in sitting postures' makes it seem more horrific.
- Empathy with the real emotions of the people who died: 'show their attitudes'.
- A sense of lives unfulfilled: 'like shadows'.
- The name 'JULIE DI DIOMEDE' gives a sense of identity.
- Language choices such as 'mortal terror' and 'wild despair' give a sense of terror.

Overall:

- The people seem real to the reader.
- Feels like the people live on and are immortalised in death.
- Respect for the Romans who faced the volcano.
- The idea that we are not so brave today – almost humorous.

This is not a checklist and the question must be marked in levels of response.

Look for and reward valid alternatives.

Unit 11
Evaluating critically

LEARNING OBJECTIVES

▶ To develop a clear understanding of what it means to 'evaluate critically'
▶ To think about a clear approach to questions that demand critical evaluation skills

Assessment Objectives

AO4 ■ Evaluate texts critically and support this with appropriate textual references

Get going

Step 1 | Work on your skills

ACTIVITY 1

Consider the following excerpts from students' responses. They could be used as a prediction exercise before reading the text *How to be Happy Though Married* or to model assessment of answers with a class, using the mark scheme that follows.

Candidate 1

The text says that it is important to keep a house clean and that a woman (a wife) should look after her husband. This is true as they can both be healthy and free from germs and they should look after each other.

Candidate 2

It is a very misogynist perspective. It also comes across as quite patronizing ('women's lives are very dull').

Candidate 3

The text is quite difficult to read from a 21st century perspective. The views are so tightly bound to prevailing Victorian attitudes to gender and religion that it seems quite alien to us today.

The tone is highly moralistic and is imperative in tone. This makes it almost comical from today's point of view.

This question tests the ability to evaluate texts critically and support this with appropriate textual references.

0 marks	Give for responses where there is nothing worthy of credit.
1–2 marks	Give to responses that express a simple personal opinion with linked basic textual reference but struggle to engage with the text and/or the question, for example, I think he is saying that it is important to have a clean and tidy home.
3–4 marks	Give to responses that give a personal opinion supported by straightforward textual references. These responses will show limited interaction with Hardy's views, for example, I don't think it is realistic to expect women to stay home and keep house for her husband because many women today work.
5–6 marks	Give to responses that give an evaluation of the text and its effects, supported by appropriate textual references. These responses will show some critical awareness of Hardy's views, for example, I think the writer has some good advice about the benefits of a well-maintained home but a lot of things he says aren't acceptable in the twenty-first century, like 'it is the duty of a wife'.

Unit 11 Evaluating critically

7–8 marks	Give to responses that give a critical evaluation of the text and its effects, supported by well-selected textual references. They will show critical awareness and clear engagement with Hardy's views, for example, the writer provides a series of quite archaic (to us in the 21st century) views on a woman's role in marriage or the definition of marriage as exclusively between a man and a woman. He asserts that the wife needs to work to keep her man happy, as shown by the use of the word 'sweetly'.
9–10 marks	Give to responses that give a persuasive evaluation of the text and its effects, supported by convincing, well-selected examples and purposeful textual references. These responses will show engagement and involvement, where candidates take an overview to make accurate and perceptive comments on Hardy's views, for example, Hardy promotes an archaic view of a woman's role in marriage, one of perfection – 'a woman should know…' This comes across as highly moralistic and unrealistic.

Areas for evaluation:
- Running a home
- Money saving
- Family involvement
- Important to work out what is actually needed
- It makes one 'useful and generous'
- Moralising/superior/preachy tone

This is not a checklist and the question must be marked in levels of response. Look for and reward valid alternatives.

	Textual reference	My views (thoughts and feelings)
Main points/content	The text says that it is essential to have a well maintained, looked after home.	This is an unrealistic expectation.
Inference	It implies that it is a wife's duty to keep house and look after her husband.	This seems sexist and is not supported with reasons as to why this opinion is offered.
Language	'Cage' is used as an extended metaphor for the home.	The writer seems very opinionated and ready to force his/her opinions on others.
Technique	Superlatives ('cleanest, sweetest') are used to infer that a woman's home should be the best possible.	This seems melodramatic and is an overreaction.
Tone	The writer uses an imperative tone.	This comes across as bossy and belligerent. I wouldn't appreciate being told what not to wear in public.
Overview	Hardy expresses a view that is very much rooted in the 19th-century values and views of a woman's role to keep house, look after her husband and adapt seamlessly to his needs and wishes.	The writing is one sided and old fashioned in terms of women having different expectations from men.

Step 2 Practise your skills

ACTIVITY 2

Here, students need to use what they have done already in Activity 1 to begin their longer piece of writing. There are five starter sentences in the Student's Book that could be used for students who need more support.

Step 3 Challenge yourself

ACTIVITY 3

You may want to approach the *How to be Happy Though Married* text in a similar way to the 'Conduct in the Street' text.

A second question could be given to students if appropriate:

'Both texts are similar in that they represent 19th-century attitudes towards women.'

How far do you agree with this statement?

Look for similarities between the two texts based on the responses you have already written.

Reading Units

Extension Activity

This could be also used as a differentiation tool for students of different abilities in the same class.

Alternatively, it could be used as a starter activity – before reading the text – to react to the textual references out of context.

	Textual reference	My views (thoughts and feelings)
Main points/ content	Paragraph two suggests that a lady must be perfectly dressed when in public.	
Inference	Women should not attract attention to themselves.	
Language	Superlative phrases such as 'Nothing looks worse' gives a sense of how important these issues are to the writer.	
Devices	Outrage is suggested through exaggeration, as if some things are a source of personal pain ('oh! spare my nerves!')	
Tone	The writer uses an imperative tone ('Wear no jewelry…'. This tries to be commanding.	
Overview	Hartley tries to convince the reader that there are right and wrong ways of a 'lady' conducting herself in the street. She commands the reader and attempts to make her opinions sound like facts.	

Improve your skills

LEARNING OBJECTIVES

- To explore critical evaluation in terms of bias
- To consider unsupported statements
- To explore approaches to questions that ask you to consider a statement about a text

Step 1 Work on your skills

ACTIVITY 1

Students could be provided with a copy of the text extract on which they can add highlighting to help them identify the features.

Below is a more developed list of features about the task in this section.

- A statement by the writer, backed up with evidence
- A statement by the writer, not backed with relevant evidence
- The views and attitudes of society at the time the text was written or set

Types of bias	Example from the text
A statement by the writer, backed up with evidence	The dead woman was named Polly and shared a room with three other women at the lodging house. (Women's evidence)
A statement by the writer, not backed up with relevant evidence	This was a murder of the 'foulest kind'.
The views and attitudes of society at the time the text was written or set	At the time, the poor were looked down upon and treated as criminals.

Unit 11 Evaluating critically

Step 2 | Practise your skills

ACTIVITY 2

Possible ideas to explore with students include:
- Biases held by you about the topic
- Biases held by the writer about the topic
- Your own thoughts and feelings
- The views/attitudes of society today
- Knowledge of other texts/references of the time

Some points that candidates may explore in terms of their thoughts and feelings:

- She talks about the way the policeman looks 'real hard' at her.
- They are never polite/no 'small' talk.
- The questions they ask sound like accusations.
- They presume the children are doing wrong – 'Who unlocked the park gate?'
- The big policeman 'snarls' his question – suggests an aggressive attitude.
- The policeman acts like a tough guy in a film – the gesture may appear threatening.
- The policeman approaches Manny, saying, 'I'm talking to you', demanding an answer – he may be deliberately confrontational.
- He grabs the ball from Manny.
- With no provocation he slaps Manny's head.
- He is racist in the way he calls him 'black boy'.
- Their behaviour makes her feel defensive towards Manny ('Manny was my brother at that moment').
- The police become 'the enemy' to the girl.
- The other policeman calls the girl 'sister' in an insulting way and threatens to arrest her.
- He then patronises her by calling her 'little girl' and Manny's girlfriend.

Types of bias	Example from the text
Biases held by you about the topic	Comments are likely to be along the lines of: I hate any form of racism; I hate bullying behaviour; I dislike people abusing their power. These can then be linked to the policemen's behaviour in the extract.
Biases held by the writer about the topic	The writer also apparently dislikes bullying and racism as she makes the policemen dislikeable. Through the narrator, we see how she sticks up for Manny.
Your own thoughts and feelings	I empathise with the main character when she sticks up for Manny as the way the policemen behave makes me angry.
The views/attitudes of society today	Unfortunately, there are still examples of racist behaviour in society today. Fortunately, these seem to be on the decrease. It also would not be acceptable for police to behave in this way and there is a big backlash against corruption and poor behaviour by people in positions of authority.
Knowledge of other texts/references of the time	The language and references to basketball in the text suggest this is America, possibly in the past. Texts such as *Of Mice and Men* and *To Kill a Mockingbird* remind us that America was a deeply racist place and, to some degree, this is referenced in the text.

Step 3 | Challenge yourself

ACTIVITY 3

This activity is intended to consolidate the learning in this unit.

Below is the completed table with suggested answers.

	Negative view of sailing	Positive view of sailing
Content (main points)	Five British yachtsmen were 'held for a week in Iran' which emphasises the danger you can get in.	People have been sailing 'for fun for over a century'. This shows that many people have done it.
Inferences	The phrase 'getting lost on the water' implies that mistakes do happen.	'Superb levels of communications' implies it is a safe thing to do.

73

Reading Units

Language	'not-so-beautiful' in the heading emphasises that the reality may not be as romantic as pictured.	'exciting escapade' creates a positive picture of adventure.
Techniques	Use of a question as a side heading ('So why bother?') emphasises the doubts.	The use of humour as in 'Appealing or appalling?' downplays the danger as not too serious.
Bias	The writer asserts that it is 'presumably faster, cheaper and simpler' to fly but doesn't really back this up with evidence.	Quotes from people who have positive views on the topic are used. ('Nothing will put me off.')

Extension Activity

This is a further text that could be used in the same way as the sailing text in Activity 3 to consolidate learning.

Students could fill in a similar table for this text, with negative and positive views of Wales. You could potentially use this as a whole class activity, where students take it in turns to fill in evidence in the grid.

'In this article, the writer portrays a negative view about Wales.'

To what extent do you agree with this view?

You should comment on:
- what is said
- how it is said.

You must refer to the text to support your comments. [10]

What sums up Wales for holidaymakers? Many of us might say rainy trips away, spent cowering under roof or canvas, cursing damp sheep, searching vainly for something decent to eat that did not involve sad flat scones filled with burnt raisins. Sad towns is another: four of Wales's conurbations – Merthyr, Swansea, Rhyl and Wrexham – appeared in 'Crap Towns Returns', a second edition of a book of supposedly the worst places in Britain.

But it's time for a re-think. In the past year or so, Wales has undoubtedly got much cooler. Whether because of conscious regeneration and rebranding – and there are some heavyweight PRs at play – or because Wales was always really rather glorious – more and more reasons are emerging to drive west.

Last week I was the first national journalist to eat at Coast at Saundersfoot, a new restaurant overlooking the beach at this pleasant fishing town, a quieter younger sister to Tenby. Although the town is British seaside defined – including 'Mini Miami' arcade games and the smell of fried food – the restaurant, which opened this spring and is set back from the tourist tat next to Coppet Hall beach, is a wholly different catch.

Will Holland, the head chef, earned a Michelin star for his former restaurant, La Becasse in Ludlow, before he was 30. He now serves a fresh, modern menu that includes fish landed at the harbour (500m away, visible from the restaurant terrace), with dishes such as crispy pigs' ears with apple sauce, grilled sea trout fillet, sweet chilli jam and lime, and poached peach with vanilla ice cream and meringue.

The room has slick wooden furniture, copper lampshades, and a sun-yourself terrace. It's not exactly budget beach fare – mains are from £13, with most of the fish dishes around £18 – but for the quality and thoughtful presentation it represents good value.

From 'How Wales got cool' by Lizzie Porter, The *Telegraph* travel website

BE EXAM READY

LEARNING OBJECTIVES

▶ To adopt a confident approach to answering exam questions that assess critical evaluation
▶ To feel confident about writing under timed conditions
▶ To apply the mark scheme with confidence

Question 1

Remind students that they have 15 minutes to answer this exam-style question.

They can then use the mark scheme provided below and in the Student's Book to assess their answer. Students should remember that this question tests the ability to evaluate texts critically and support this with appropriate textual references.

1–2 marks	• Simple personal opinion, for example: I think he is saying that South Wales is not a nice place to visit. • Little or no textual evidence for support
3–4 marks	• Some personal opinion • Straightforward textual references • Basic interaction with the statement, for example: I do agree with the statement because he describes the industry in a lot of detail and it sounds very dirty and dismal.
5–6 marks	• Clear discussion of the text and its effects • Appropriate textual references • Discussion and some evaluation of the statement, for example: I think the statement is correct to an extent, as he does use some critical language to describe the area. For example, he refers to the chimneys and 'grimy' and focuses on the 'cinders' and 'black rubbish'. This all gives a negative effect.
7–8 marks	• Critical evaluation of the text and its effects • Well-selected textual references • Clear engagement with the statement, for example: The statement does have some truth to it, as the writer does focus on the negative effect of the industry in the area at the time. He uses negative words and imagery to describe the place ('smoke' and 'Diabolical') and even compares it to Hell. However, there are positives in the account too, and Borrow seems to separate out the industry from the surrounding area: e.g. the 'majestic' hills.
9–10 marks	• Persuasive evaluation of the text and its effects • Convincing, well-selected examples and purposeful textual references • Perceptive comments on the statement and the text as a whole, for example: Borrow has a tone of wonder and amazement – the whole thing seems 'extraordinary' to him, as if it is the work of imagination (emphasised by the reference to the painter Jerome Bos).

Possible areas for evaluation could include:

- At first, the area sounds pleasant: 'village', 'wooded height'.
- The view comes as a shock – 'extraordinary'.
- The scale of it is 'immense'.
- It sounds dirty ('grimy') and uninviting.
- There is a sense of confusion ('pandemonium') and death ('choking').
- He builds upon the sense of disgust with image after image of disgust.
- Vision of Hell
- The passer-by is friendly and answers his questions.
- The abbey is difficult to get to.
- It stands in a meadow/surrounded by majestic hills.
- The ruin itself is talked about in positive terms – 'mighty vault' and 'beautiful pillars'.
- He does not stay long.
- He is not used to the industry of the time.
- A snapshot – we don't know what else he chronicles

This is not a checklist. Valid alternatives will also be rewarded.

The following are commentaries on the candidates answers that appear in the Student's Book.

Commentary on candidate 1's answer

Simple personal opinions and some very brief references to the text. 2 marks.

75

Reading Units

Commentary on candidate 2's answer

Clear discussion of the text with some textual references to back up opinions. Mostly, the textual details are well chosen. The exploration of Devil, the discussion of the effect of the size and discussion of the tone gets this response to 7 marks.

Commentary on candidate 3's answer

Perceptive discussion of the texts with precise textual references to support. Confident discussion of the techniques in the text (such as language contrasts) and probing of the images. 10 marks.

You may then choose to provide students with the partner text that would appear in the exam and ask them to answer the following question:

'This extract portrays a positive view of Wales.'

To what extent do you agree with this view?

You should comment on:

- **what is said**
- **how it is said.**

You must refer to the text to support your comments. [10]

How green are our Valleys? ... VERY!

If your view of The Valleys is an area of coal mines and scarred landscapes – then take another look. The Valleys are green – with forests, country parks, unspoilt hillsides, open common land, clear rivers and crisp lakes together providing a wonderful backdrop to the traditional Valley communities.

Getting out into The Valleys is all about refreshing your spirit – a great way to help cope with the everyday pressures of life. All you need to do is to pull on your walking boots and follow some of the inspired routes that link communities and hillsides – how about exploring Twmbarlwm, our very own Bronze Age hill fort with spectacular views across The Bristol Channel, or discover the native residents of Swiss Valley near Llanelli. There are also great circular routes around Pontypridd and for the really adventurous, how about stepping out from the north to the south of The Valleys on the Taff Trail, Rhymney or Sirhowy Valley Trails. You could choose a different route each weekend and still have new ones to discover at the end of 2014!

"This is spectacular countryside. Buzzards wheeling around overhead, air so fresh it feels restorative, and vast open space where you can quickly lose yourself in your thoughts. If you're into walking there's a multitude of routes you can take depending on how long you've got or how challenging you want to make your adventure. Plus there's a few pubs dotted around that are worth factoring in to your itinerary."

Gareth Johnson, *Gay Star News*

Waterfall Country

'I cannot call to mind a single valley that in the same extent of country comprises so much beautiful and picturesque scenery and so many interesting and special features as the Vale of Neath.'

That's what the famous 19th Century naturalist Alfred Russel Wallace wrote when he first experienced the Vale of Neath. He summed it up pretty well. Waterfall Country is a hidden treasure, a sequence of striking waterfalls that ensure that walks in this area are truly memorable – especially if you are able to venture behind Sgwd yr Eira – and experience the noise and power of water forming a living curtain in front of you!

Students should use the mark scheme below to think about their answer. Remember that this question tests the ability to evaluate texts critically and support this with appropriate textual references.

1–2 marks	• Simple personal opinion, for example: I think he is saying that South Wales is a nice place to visit.' • Little or no textual evidence for support
3–4 marks	• Some personal opinion • Straightforward textual references • Basic interaction with the statement, for example: I do agree with the statement because he describes all the positives about the area such as the waterfalls and scenery.
5–6 marks	• Clear discussion of the text and its effects • Appropriate textual references • Discussion and some evaluation of the statement, for example: I think the statement is correct, as the writer uses some positive language to describe the area. For example, he refers to the 'unspoilt hillsides' and 'spectacular' scenery which gives a positive effect.
7–8 marks	• Critical evaluation of the text and its effects • Well-selected textual references • Clear engagement with the statement, for example: The statement does have some truth to it, as the writer does focus on the positives of the South Wales scenery. He suggests that the reader pulls on their 'walking boots', however this might imply that there is a lot of effort needed in exploring this area, which might not be a positive thing.
9–10 marks	• Persuasive evaluation of the text and its effects • Convincing, well-selected examples and purposeful textual references • Perceptive comments on the statement and the text as a whole, for example: The text has a tone of wonder and amazement – the metaphor of the waterfall forming a 'living curtain' sounds like the scenery is throbbing with life.

Extension Activity

This is a second text that could be used with a similar exam-style question for extra practice. Students or teachers can use the same mark scheme above.

> Durham village of Easington where film, Billy Elliot, was made gets special mention as performance of musical is beamed to cinemas
>
> Almost everyone in Easington has a Billy Elliot story. One man claims to have received Billy's bed from the props department after it was vacated by Jamie Bell, a local lad from nearby Billingham, who beat thousands of hopefuls to win the title role in the film. One lady remembers fake snow blocking the drains in her terraced street long after the crew had packed up in 1999.
>
> But Sally Miller has a special claim to fame. Her husband, 52-year-old former miner Michael, was actually in it. 'He played a policeman,' she said proudly. 'He was between jobs at the time and he saw it advertised in the local jobcentre so thought he'd get a few days work out of it.'
>
> On Sunday night the Millers were among 220 people from the onetime pit village in County Durham who packed into the Easington Social Centre, formerly the Colliery Miners' Institute, for a very special show.
>
> The hall, a focal point for the community during the crippling 1980s strikes portrayed in the film, had been turned into a cinema, and satellite equipment had been installed on the roof so that a performance of Billy Elliot the Musical – the West End spinoff of the movie – could be beamed live into the village where the film was made, as well as to 550 cinemas in the UK and worldwide.
>
> Almost 10 million people around the world have now seen the stage show about the 11-year-old miner's son who dreams of being a ballerina. But many in Easington, including the 400-odd locals who ended up as extras, have never made it down to London, let alone Broadway, to experience it live.

Reading Units

Sunday's linkup was the next best thing, with the audience roaring with delight when Stephen Daldry, the show's director, gave them a special mention before the curtain call. 'We salute the people of Easington and welcome them to our show,' he said to cheers. Tickets for the Easington screening cost £1, subsidised by the stage show's producers.

No one in Easington realised that the film they watched being made at the end of their streets at the end of the last millennium would turn into a worldwide hit that would be nominated for three Oscars. Nor did Jon Finn, one of the film's producers, from Gateshead. 'We thought we were making a small film. We didn't expect it to do anything,' he said.

Finn remembers that Easington locals were 'slightly sceptical, but all very warm'. Filming went smoothly but for one unfortunate night shoot. 'The only time we almost came to blows was when we were shooting a night scene up at the allotments and a lighting tower crushed a bed of leeks. I can't tell you how much upset that caused. It was the night before the giant vegetable competition, which is taken very seriously round those parts. I ended up paying the guy £2,000 compensation. I think they'd have been less upset if we'd crushed a baby.'

Most people in Easington are enormously proud of the village's association with Billy Elliot. There's a proposal to commission a statue of Billy jumping in the air, said local county councillor David Boyes, who is among many in the village to claim that his old street was the site of Billy's tap dance to the Jam's 'Town Called Malice'.

'It's fantastic that a big hit film was made in Easington. We feel very lucky,' Boyes said. 'But the premise of the film is a different matter entirely. The idea that Billy was only going to achieve fulfilment by leaving a community like ours and heading for the bright lights of London – I take issue with that. I have heard moaning that we are not as culturally backwards round here as the film made out.'

Usually, articles about Easington mention its unenviable position at the bottom of all too many league tables, whether for health outcomes, obesity rates or joblessness. It is regularly singled out as one of the most deprived areas of the country, with unemployment currently at 10.8%.

'A lot of bad things have been written about us here,' said Angela Surtees, another councillor. 'So it was nice for the world to see somebody from a working class community like ours actually making something of themselves.'

From *The Guardian* online

'The website article does not present a favourable view of Easingdon and its people.'

To what extent do you agree with this view?

You should comment on:

- **what is said**
- **how it is said.**

You must refer to the text to support your comments. [10]

Points that could be explored:

- Generalises: 'Almost everyone' in Easington has a *Billy Elliot* story.
- Interesting stories about the making of the film can be found there ('fake snow blocking the drains').
- Some residents were in the film – a direct link.
- Suggests lots of unemployment ('former miner'/'between jobs'/'local jobcentre').

- 'the onetime pit village'.
- 'Easington Social Centre' could be perceived as a strong community.
- 'crippling' suggests that they were badly injured by the strikes.
- 'turned into a cinema' might suggest a lack of facilities.
- 'satellite equipment had been installed on the roof' shows there is investment in the village.
- '10 million people around the world have now seen the stage show' – wide recognition and fame of the village.
- 'many in Easington, have never made it down to London' suggests that the people are not widely travelled.
- 'special mention' – they are worthy of singling out.
- 'subsidised' by the stage show's producers (could be positive or negative).
- 'locals were all 'very warm'. Shows friendly, welcoming people.
- 'the giant vegetable competition, which is taken very seriously'. Sounds a bit patronising – as if there is nothing better to do.
- 'Proposal to commission a statue of Billy' – there is a pride in the association with the film.
- 'We feel very lucky'.
- Promotes the idea that people are 'culturally backwards'.
- 'unenviable' position in terms of league tables.
- 'bottom' for health outcomes, obesity rates or joblessness.
- 'one of the most deprived areas of the country' – negative statistic.
- 'somebody from a working class community like ours actually making something of themselves' – ends on a positive, but makes it sound unusual.

Unit 12
Communicating clearly and effectively

LEARNING OBJECTIVES

▶ To learn to present your ideas clearly and effectively
▶ To improve your technical accuracy

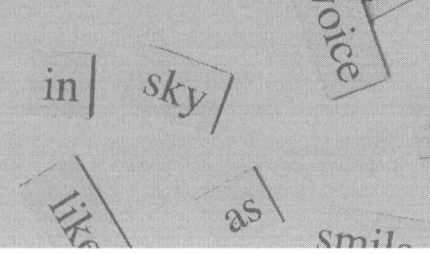

Assessment Objectives

AO5 ■ Communicate clearly, effectively and imaginatively selecting and adapting tone, style and register for different forms, purposes and audiences.
■ Organise information and ideas to support coherence and cohesion of texts using structural and grammatical features.
AO6 ■ Use a range of vocabulary and sentence structure for clarity, purpose and effect with accurate spelling and punctuation.

You could begin by taking students through the section on Assessment Objectives to allay their fears and go through the simplified version so they understand exactly what they are being asked to do in straightforward terms.

Read the Top tips box with students.

Get going

Step 1 Work on your skills

ACTIVITY 1

Revise what a paragraph is and why they are used.

You could model a paragraph on the board to help students begin this activity. Go over their responses, possibly as a class, when they have finished.

ACTIVITY 2

Encourage students to use connectives to organise and link their ideas.

Ask them to think of what persuasive devices they might want to include to make the argument more convincing and persuasive. You should be looking for:

- exclamations
- rhetorical questions
- emotive vocabulary
- ellipses
- expert opinion, etc.

Ask students to read their responses aloud so the class can decide on the most persuasive attempt.

ACTIVITY 3

In pairs, ask students to read the reviews and decide where the paragraphs should begin. Here are the answers they might suggest:

Review 1
- 'Looking for some thrills…'
- 'Wuthering Heights' by Emily Brontë…'
- 'If you're hooked by gothic…'

Go over the responses and encourage students to explain their decisions.

Review 2
- 'At first glance…'
- 'Fancy a more active holiday?'
- 'Mauritius has a wealth of natural history…'
- 'Also dotted around…'

Go over responses and encourage students to explain their decisions.

80

Unit 12 Communicating clearly and effectively

ACTIVITY 4

Explain to the students that paragraphs help to organise a writer's thoughts and ideas.

Ask them to write a few paragraphs about each of the listed topics to practise this skill. Encourage the use of connectives. Go over responses, perhaps as a class.

ACTIVITY 5

To practise this skill further, this activity asks students to read the jumbled paragraphs about the dangers of mobile phones and arrange them in the best order.

They might suggest this structure:

1 'We have managed…'
2 'Only last week…'
3 'Teenagers are stealing…'
4 'Furthermore,…'
5 'Text messaging…'
6 'In conclusion,…'
7 'Thank you…'

ACTIVITY 6

Explain to students what a **topic** or **focus** sentence is and its importance. Read the example with them and ask them to write a paragraph that could follow on. Go over and discuss responses, looking in particular for paragraphs that are focused with a clear link back to the topic sentence.

To consolidate this skill, ask students to write a topic sentence and paragraph on each subject in the list. You could model the first one and ask students to continue, if students require more support. Look for responses where the outline is clear and every word supports the point that is being made.

ACTIVITY 7

Go over the rules of punctuating direct speech with students and ask them to find six paragraphs in the extract from 'Help' and to be able to explain their decisions. Here are the answers they might suggest:

- Henry said,…
- But none the less…
- 'You'll have to get some help.'
- Guiltily,…
- 'I'd feel awkward…'
- He brushed…

Next ask students to read the extract from *Of Mice and Men* and identify five paragraphs and explain their choices. Here are the answers they might suggest:

- Although there was evening…
- Slim and George…
- 'It wasn't nothing…'
- George said,…
- 'It wasn't nothing…'

Go over and discuss responses and reasons for choices. They should be able to back up their choices with evidence.

Remind students about the points in the Top tips box and draw their attention to the range of different connectives given in the table.

ACTIVITIES 8 AND 9

Both these activities embed and consolidate the use of connectives. Activity 9 encourages students to be selective in their use of topic sentences. Activity 10 consolidates the learning by having them write an article for a magazine. Students should be encouraged to note that magazine articles are often short and snappy.

ACTIVITY 10

Encourage students to use redrafting skills to improve this paragraph. You could model the rewriting of the first example and then encourage students to continue the task. Spend some time going over and discussing word and punctuation choices.

Step 2 Practise your skills

ACTIVITIES 11–16

These activities are short exercises to allow students to explore the use of different kinds of sentences. Modelling types of sentences before students approach the relevant activity would help.

Activity 15 asks students to identify the different types of sentences in this list. Here are possible responses:

a Compound
b Simple
c Simple
d Complex
e Compound
f Minor

Writing Units

Spend time discussing responses.

Activity 16 develops students' understanding and confidence, and asks students to write a series of paragraphs using connectives and containing a range of sentence types.

They could swap responses with a partner to highlight the different types of sentences.

ACTIVITY 17

In pairs ask students to read the extract, then find and identify different types of sentences. Here are some areas they might explore:

- 'Guilt' – minor
- 'I never liked that feeling.' – simple
- 'I knew I was wrong…' – complex
- 'I just couldn't…' – compound
- 'Although…' – complex

Perhaps the sentence with most impact would be 'Although I had to run, I wondered what would happen when they found me' – because it creates suspense/tension/mystery: who are they?

Then encourage students to write another page as a continuation to this opening paragraph.

ACTIVITY 18

Here are some points students might come up with:

- Minor – 'Yes, the wolf.', 'Evil and vicious?', 'Not so.'
- Simple – 'Any idea who this creature can be?'
- Compound – 'I am here tonight…', 'Now we have grown up…'
- Complex – 'When we were little…'

Go over the responses and have students write another two or three paragraphs to continue the speech, making sure they use different kinds of sentences.

ACTIVITY 19

Explain to students how they can expand the sentences they write by using adjectives, adverbs and prepositions. Ask them to look at the table containing different parts of speech.

a Ask students to create sentences from the words, choosing one from each column. Let them have some fun making up silly sentences.

b Ask students to choose and read out three of their best sentences. Class feedback could be interesting here!

c Ask students to change some words so sentences are sensible. Go over these responses.

d Students should write five more sentences of their own using all the parts of speech in the columns. Go over responses.

Draw students' attention to the information in the Top tips box about using short sentences for impact.

Step 3 | Challenge yourself

Explain the introductory section about different ways to start a sentence in order to create variety/effect.

ACTIVITY 20

Ask students to read the extract and identify different ways of starting sentences. Here are some suggested responses:

- Pronoun starter – I felt…; I screamed…
- Definite article starter – The window…
- Preposition starter – Behind me…
- -ing participle starter – Peering over…
- Adjective starter – Cold beads…
- Adverb starter – Slowly…
- Connective starter – Although…
- Verb starter – To run

ACTIVITY 21

Read the article about footballers' wages. Students might suggest the following points that the article does well:

- Ambitious vocabulary – 'unjust', 'scandalous', 'valuing'
- Use of exclamations to suggest shock or outrage
- Sensible ideas

Then ask them to identify an area for improvement. They should notice that too many sentences begin with the pronoun 'I'.

Ask students to rewrite the paragraph by varying the beginning of the sentences. Go over finished responses. Then encourage students to select their favourite sentence and ask them to explain their choices.

Unit 12 Communicating clearly and effectively

ACTIVITY 22

Students read the student text and decide whether it is boring and predictable. They should decide that it is not, because of the variety of techniques and sentence starters:

- Definite and indefinite article starters
- Preposition starter
- Noun starter
- Pronoun starter

ACTIVITY 23

Students should work independently to write about their childhood memories with a focus on varying the type of sentences and sentence starters they use.

When these are finished, they provide an opportunity for peer-/self-assessment.

Ask students to identify the different types of sentence and sentence starters they have used.

Encourage them to identify two things they are pleased with and two things they still need to improve upon. Go over responses. These should be their targets for their next piece of writing.

Improve your skills

LEARNING OBJECTIVES

▶ To make my writing more accurate technically
▶ To use apostrophes correctly
▶ To learn to proof read my work effectively

Explain about the importance of learning to spell accurately, not just in English exams, but in a range of other subjects as well.

Step 1 Work on your skills

ACTIVITY 1

Suggest some spelling strategies to the students and go through the homophone exercise. Here are the answers students should come up with:

1 Hear	4 Their	7 See
2 Wood	5 Know	8 Right
3 Blew	6 Chews	9 Reign

Go over the responses and encourage students to write a sentence for each of the homophones not used in the above exercise. Spend time discussing and collating responses.

Next, ask students to think of another five commonly confused homophones. Here are a few they might think of:

- beach/beech
- pour/poor/paw/pore
- caught/court
- peek/peak
- steal/steel

Go over responses and ask students to explain the different meanings of their choices

ACTIVITY 2

Ask students to read the following extract and find and correct the homophones that have been confused.

Answers

- Deer (dear)
- Right (write)
- Ewe (you)
- Chews (choose)
- Right (write)
- Knot (not)
- Two (to)
- Too (to)
- Ewe (you)
- Seeside (seaside)
- Grate (great)
- Blew (blue)
- See (sea)
- Weigh (way)
- Hear (here)
- Ewe (you)
- To (too)

83

Writing Units

ACTIVITY 3

Encourage students to complete this spelling challenge and decide which word has been written correctly.

Answers
- definite
- disappoint
- terrified
- disastrous
- argument

ACTIVITY 4

Introduce students to the idea of using a mnemonic as a strategy for learning to spell a tricky word. They may already be familiar with this strategy, so there may be no need to spend too long on these activities.

Begin by asking them if they know any already, and model these on the board.

Students will probably find the following words within words:

- Secretary – secret – a secretary keeps a 'secret'
- Separate – a rat – there is always 'a rat' in separate
- Soldier – sold – old – die – an old soldier will die
- Believe – lie – never believe a lie
- Business – bus – in – there is always a bus in business

ACTIVITY 5

In pairs students create mnemonics or silly rules to remember the following spellings – definitely, parliament, embarrass. Examples are:

- Definitely – there's always a 'nit' in definitely.
- Parliament – Liam goes to parliament.
- Embarrass – every mother's boy acts rather rudely after some sausages.

Then encourage students to think of three words of their own choice that they are not always confident about spelling correctly. Go over these responses.

ACTIVITY 6

This could be an independent and individual writing task. Students should write about a place they are familiar with (somewhere often visited, a favourite place or a favourite room in the house). The focus should be on using paragraphs, connectives, varied sentence structure and sentence starters and spelling. Share responses with the class.

Step 2 Practise your skills

Explain or remind students about the two uses for apostrophes – possession and omission.

ACTIVITY 7

An initial activity to help students remember how to use apostrophes correctly is to rewrite the signs given in the Student's Book.

Answers
- Farm fresh carrots and potatoes for sale
- Men's department on the second floor
- Year 10 Parents' Evening
- Children's Play Area at rear of pub
- Slimmers' Club. New Members Are Welcome!
- Party Aces! Let's Plan All Your Parties
- Holiday Cottages For Rent. Apply Within.

ACTIVITY 8

To embed and consolidate understanding of apostrophes, ask students to read the following paragraph and put in the missing apostrophes, saying whether it is because of possession or omission.

Answers
- Tom's – possession
- hadn't – omission
- would've – omission
- life's – possession
- dad's – possession
- men's – possession
- he'd – omission
- family's – possession
- uncle's – possession
- firm's – possession
- neighbours' – possession
- Independent's – possession
- women's – possession
- what's – omission

Unit 12 Communicating clearly and effectively

ACTIVITY 9

This activity is an important introduction to proofreading work – which they should begin to use in their own work!

They should identify the errors in spelling, punctuation and expression. Here are some areas they might focus on:

- Im (I'm)
- on that (about whether)
- inn (in)
- outdorr activitys (outdoor activities)
- As I and fellow pupils has took a query around (My fellow pupils and I conducted a survey)
- very much big percentage (a large percentage)
- becasuse (because)
- most pupils' (most pupils)
- it would take the strass (it would keep the stress)
- the final sentence (The class has suggested that those people who have made the biggest contribution to school life, as shown by their behaviour or number of award stickers, should be chosen.)

ACTIVITY 10

Read the magazine article about fashion and ask students to come up with two things the answer does well. They might suggest the following points: lively tone; uses a range of techniques such as ellipses, rhetorical questions, adjectives; vocabulary is ambitious.

Next is an opportunity for independent and individual writing. Students should write their own answer to the question with a focus on technical accuracy including paragraphs, spelling, sentence types, sentence structure, etc.

This is an opportunity for peer-/self-assessment.

Spend some time going through the Top tips box and reinforcing the need for students to proofread their work carefully.

Step 3 Challenge yourself

ACTIVITY 11

Ask students to proofread the letter about raising the legal driving age and to make corrections.

Answers
- im (I'm)
- wrighting (writing)
- payed (paid)
- there (their)
- sensaball (sensibly)
- strrets (streets)
- thay (they)
- there (their)
- there (they're)
- psying (paying)
- senscelly (sincerely)

Then students should rewrite the letter using their own ideas and the skills they have been practising in this unit.

When they have finished, encourage them to assess their work using the list in the Student's Book.

ACTIVITY 12

Ask students to write about a family occasion they remember well making use of the skills they have been practising.

Give students some time to complete the '… do you think your confidence has increased?' table to ascertain whether their skills and confidence have increased during this section.

BE EXAM READY

LEARNING OBJECTIVES

▶ To use vocabulary effectively and precisely
▶ To feel confident about writing accurately

Take students through the opening paragraph to make them aware of the importance of using precise and specific vocabulary to create effect. Re-introduce them to using synonyms.

Question 1

In pairs, and using a thesaurus, ask students to find alternative word choices for the following five words.

Here it would be worth discussing the different connotations of each word choice and the type of situation it might be most suitable for.

Answers

a shouted – yelled; called out; cried; bawled; yelped; screamed; shrieked
b old – elderly; ancient; mature; antiquated; threadbare; tattered; worn out; moth eaten
c opinion – belief; judgement; viewpoint; angle; outlook; perspective; position
d nasty – unpleasant; disgusting; awful; sickening; revolting; horrible; filthy
e nice – pleasant; charming; delightful; amiable; friendly

Question 2

For this question, encourage students to decide why the letter sounds boring. Hopefully they will point out that the word 'got' has been overused and that it lacks precision.

Either individually or in pairs students should use a thesaurus to find more appropriate alternatives for the word 'got'. Spend some time going over and discussing valid alternatives.

You could suggest the following:

1 arrived at; 2 were shocked/received; 3 be forced to/had to; 4 entered; 5 find/prepare; 6 reached; 7 bring/serve; 8 reach; 9 receive; 10 becoming/feeling; 11 achieve anything/help us; 12 escape/leave; 13 returned; 14 been scratched; 15 receiving; 16 involving

Question 3

Ask students to write their own letter of complaint to the manager of a restaurant where they have experienced a disastrous meal and poor service. They should be encouraged to organise their ideas effectively and think carefully about their word choices.

Spend time listening to responses and discussing ideas and word choices.

Question 4

Ask students, in pairs, to rearrange the list of synonyms for the word 'tragic' in order from least 'tragic' to most 'tragic'. Here are some possible suggestions they might make:

- unfortunate – awful – terrible – dreadful – disastrous – devastating – horrendous – catastrophic – cataclysmic

Go over responses and ask students to explain what they perceive to be the differences between the words.

You could ask students to write a sentence using each word from the question above. Spend some time going over the responses.

Question 5

In this question, encourage students to discuss what they think of when reading the words in the Student's Book.

They may come up with these ideas, or similar:

- savagery – ferocity; brutality; wildness; cruelty
- aroma – perfume; pleasant scent
- abysmal – appalling; disgraceful; shameful

Spend some time discussing responses and reward any suitable student responses.

Unit 12 Communicating clearly and effectively

Question 6
In pairs ask students to write down their initial thoughts and responses to the provocative statement.

Then encourage them to write a couple of paragraphs in response to the statement, reminding them of the importance of choosing words carefully and using emotive language.

Spend time going over the responses.

Question 7
With the students, read the paragraph and ask them what they could do to improve the vocabulary that has been used.

They will probably suggest that some words are overused and repeated too often. Ask them to use a thesaurus to improve the word choices here. Spend some time going over and collating the answers.

Question 8
Using the previous question as a starting point for a discussion of ideas on the topic, ask students to write an article for their school/college magazine about whether or not they consider footballers to be good role models for young people.

When they have finished, they can select what they consider to be their best paragraph to read aloud. Encourage students to discuss their word choices.

Question 9
Ask students, working individually, to read the student responses in their Student's Book and use all the skills they have learnt in this unit to correct any mistakes they find.

They may come up with responses like these:

Answer 1
Some of the vocabulary is a bit 'ordinary' and could be improved/developed; for example, 'an easy place to get to'; 'a very big city'.

There are punctuation errors:
- just look out for... – Just look out for...
- were all the activiys – where all the activities
- sites are in the centre. – sites are in the centre,
- Manchesters suburban places – Manchester's suburban places
- lowry theatre – Lowry Theatre
- if you spend £5 or more – If you spend £5 or more

- old Trafford – Old Trafford
- whether its family related – whether it's family related

Answer 2
- everyones first choice – everyone's first choice
- Why stay inside watching television – Why stay inside watching television?
- Theres a wide range – There's a wide range
- its allways nice – it's always nice
- icecream – ice cream
- the Rays of the sun – the rays of the sun
- and Relax the beach is open – and relax. The beach is open
- there is also a lot of activitys – there are also a lot of activities

Ask students to explain the reason for their corrections.

Question 10
Draw the students' attention to the assessment criteria they read at the start of the unit and with these in mind, ask them to decide which of the two sample responses would score most marks. They must be able to justify/explain their decision.

They will probably decide that the first response is the most successful because it is more technically accurate and the vocabulary is more specific and ambitious.

Question 11
Now students should write their own response about a good place to visit for a day trip.

87

Writing Units

Extension Activity 1

Your school/college is planning to put on a show at the end of the year.

You are asked to give a talk encouraging students to get involved. You want to persuade as many students as possible to take part.

The show will need:

- different kinds of entertainers and performers
- stage crew, backstage helpers and students to help with ticket sales, programme design, etc.

Write what you would say.

Extension Activity 2

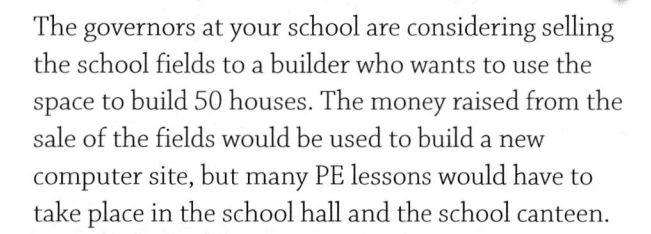

The governors at your school are considering selling the school fields to a builder who wants to use the space to build 50 houses. The money raised from the sale of the fields would be used to build a new computer site, but many PE lessons would have to take place in the school hall and the school canteen.

You have been asked to write a report about the proposal above.

Extension Activity 3

Your family has won an adventure holiday, watching animals in the wild. You are allowed to invite one of your friends.

Write a letter to your friend to explain about the holiday and try to persuade him/her to come with you.

Unit 13
Communicating imaginatively

LEARNING OBJECTIVES

▶ To be able to use words for effect
▶ To learn to write a successful opening for a creative prose response

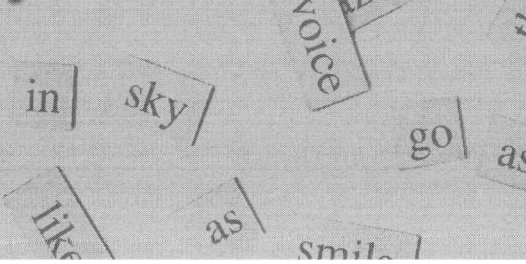

Assessment Objectives

AO5 ■ Communicate clearly, effectively and imaginatively selecting and adapting tone, style and register for different forms, purposes and audiences.
■ Organise information and ideas to support coherence and cohesion of texts using structural and grammatical features.
AO6 ■ Use a range of vocabulary and sentence structure for clarity, purpose and effect with accurate spelling and punctuation.

Read the introductory paragraph about what creative writing entails and familiarise students with the list of key terms.

Get going

Step 1 Work on your skills

ACTIVITY 1

In pairs ask students to read the list of statements about creative writing and to decide whether they are true or false.

Answers

Statement	True or false?
1 The purpose of a narrative is to persuade the reader to do something.	False
2 A narrative should be clearly and logically organised in paragraphs.	True
3 The purpose of a narrative is to provide the reader with information.	True
4 A narrative can be written in the first or third person.	True
5 The purpose of a narrative is to entertain and engage the interest of the reader.	True
6 A narrative uses subheadings.	False
7 A successful narrative should include some direct speech.	True
8 Nothing happens in a narrative – it only contains description.	False
9 A successful narrative needs a strong opening and ending.	True
10 You don't need to plan your narrative before you begin writing it.	False

Ask students about their reading habits.

- How long does it take them to decide whether they want to keep reading a story?
- What sort of opening would grab their attention and hook them?

Discuss their suggestions and comments. This could be an opportunity for the teacher to share some of his/her favourite books/story openings.

ACTIVITY 2

Ask students, in pairs, to read the story openings from a range of novels and answer the questions that follow them. Here are some answers they might suggest.

89

Writing Units

Opening A
- Yes – '7 minutes after midnight'; 'The dog was dead.'
- Yes – What had happened to the dog? Who did the dog belong to? How did the narrator come across it? Why was the dog impaled in the grass? Who did it and why?
- 'running on its side'; 'garden fork sticking out'; 'the fork had not fallen over'

Opening B
- Yes – 'It was a bright cold day in April and the clocks were striking thirteen.'
- Yes
- Yes – 'the clocks were striking thirteen'
- 'to escape the vile wind'; 'a swirl of gritty dust' (creates idea of hostile and threatening weather and surroundings assaulting the character; pathetic fallacy perhaps?); 'his chin nuzzled into his breast' (suggests he's trying to protect himself against the elements?); use of names – 'Winston Smith' (suggests he is just an ordinary, insignificant man); 'Victory Mansions' (suggests a feeling of opulence and splendour which could be ironic)

Opening C
- Yes – creates mystery and seems like an alien, futuristic or science fiction atmosphere
- 'unchartered backwaters' (suggests it is an unexplored new territory); 'a small unregarded yellow sun' (suggests it is something insignificant but this could be ironic just to lull us); 'they still think digital watches are a pretty neat idea' (creates humour)

Opening D
- Yes – How old is Prim? Why is she having bad dreams? What is 'the reaping'?
- Yes – 'This is the day of the reaping.' (sounds dangerous and ominous)
- Yes – creates interest for the reader
- It allows us to experience the events with the characters; creates a sense of immediacy and makes it dramatic

Opening E
- Yes – Who has gone? Why can't he sleep? Why is time so precious?
- The short sentences and ellipsis build suspense and tension.

Spend some time going over these answers and discussing ideas with the class.

Step 2 | Practise your skills

ACTIVITY 3

Begin by asking students to write a list of techniques they could include in an opening paragraph based on what they have learnt from the previous exercises.

Then take students through the list of techniques suggested and ask them to come up with their own examples for each one. Go over and collate examples and suggestions of these.

Ask students, in pairs, to read the following story openings and answer the questions. Here are some areas they might explore:

a 'bitterly cold'; 'chill wind'; 'swirled mercilessly'; 'grey'; 'threat of snow'

b A negative atmosphere is created with the weather being seen as hostile, threatening, cruel and ominous, almost like an enemy.

c 'Blond'; 'petite'; 'perfect pearly white'; 'wide smile'; 'icy blue'; 'brand new'; 'expensive'

d It suggests that her character isn't as nice as she appears on the surface and that there is another side to her; it implies an insincere and superficial perfection.

e These details suggest she is insincere and fake; she is quite a cold character who is hard and unfeeling; this stance suggests she could be arrogant, aggressive, confrontational ad confident.

f No

g To improve, descriptive details and adjectives could be added, less boring verbs could be used and dialogue could be included.

h The questions hook the reader's curiosity. They create a sense of regret and desperation. We want to know what has happened in the past.

i Traumatised by the incident? A victim of some sort? Haunted by the event? Guilty?

j Questions and an ellipsis are used to suggest suspense and tension.

k The mood is one of violence and aggression; also of regret and shame.

Spend some time discussing and going over these answers and suggestions.

Unit 13 Communicating imaginatively

ACTIVITY 4

Ask students to write the opening paragraph for the familiar fairy stories concentrating on some of the techniques they have learnt.

Spend some time sharing and discussing ideas when they have finished.

ACTIVITY 5

Ask students to study the pictures and to decide:

- what they think is going on
- what is suggested about the characters and relationships between them
- what the characters could be thinking/feeling/saying.

Go over these suggestions.

Ask students to write an interesting opening paragraph for each picture, using the techniques they have been practising. You could model an example on the board to give the students confidence and guidance. When they have completed their own versions, share the good practice around the class.

This provides an opportunity for peer-/self-assessment. Ask students to swap with a partner or to carefully re-read their own work. Encourage them to underline/highlight any interesting words/phrases they have used. Ask them to think about what impressions they have created of character and setting. Spend some time going over these answers.

Now ask students to write down two things they are pleased with. Go through these together.

Next ask students to write down two things they need to improve upon when they write an opening paragraph in future. Go over these responses and use them as targets for the next piece of writing.

Step 3 Challenge yourself

Explain to students that they need to reassess and re-evaluate their writing in order to improve and score higher marks. To encourage them to do this you could show them how famous authors have redrafted their work in order to improve it.

The Student's Book tells them how Owen's initial thoughts changed and gradually evolved before he was satisfied with the final version.

Ask students to select some of the changes between Owen's original and final versions and to think about why the final version is more successful. Discuss responses and ideas here.

Next, take the students through the points relating to redrafting and the Top tips box.

ACTIVITY 6

Ask students to look at the opening paragraph about the seaside and to think about why it needs to be improved. They should try to come up with three possible areas for improvement.

Here are some aspects they might explore:
- Lack of description
- No adjectives or adverbs
- No development of ideas
- No dialogue
- No variety in sentence construction or sentence length

Now, they should look at the second version of the same opening and pick out any interesting descriptive details.

Here are some points they might make:
- 'plain red dress'
- 'white with sun cream'
- 'shimmering golden sands'
- 'dancing blue sea'

A nostalgic and wistful atmosphere of memories and reminiscence is created by some of these details; 'I was never to go again'; 'I saw through a child's eyes and fondly remember'.

Spend some time going over and discussing these responses.

Finish by asking students to write an opening for a creative response entitled 'Memories of the Seaside'. Spend some time reading them out in class and discussing different ideas, word choices and approaches.

ACTIVITY 7

Next, read the story opening about an embarrassing moment with the students. Ask students what could be done to make it more interesting and entertaining to read. They might consider some of these points:

- Dialogue
- Description
- Sound effects
- Exclamations
- Reflective questions

91

Writing Units

You could model an example of a more interesting opening using the techniques the students have been practising. Then students should be encouraged to write their own version of this incident or a similar embarrassing moment. Spend some time going over the responses.

ACTIVITY 8

Then ask students, individually, to write an entertaining opening for each of the three titles, practising the techniques they have been learning about.

This provides an opportunity for peer-/self-assessment and students should be encouraged to look for any areas in their work to redraft or edit.

Ensure that students understand the advice and points about how to improve their work in the key terms and Top tips boxes.

Improve your skills

LEARNING OBJECTIVES

▶ To organise a coherent story line
▶ To practise creating characters and setting effectively

Begin by asking students to come up with what they think the 'ingredients' of a successful story would be in terms of structure. Collate answers and suggestions and compare these with the suggested list in the Top tips box.

Introduce students to the five-point plan for writing stories.

Step 1 | Work on your skills

ACTIVITY 1

Ask students, using this five-point plan structure, to work at producing a five-point plan for the list of five creative writing titles.

Allow them to create the plan in whatever format is most helpful to them. You could draw students' attention to the example of the diagram as a model for them to follow. Alternately, you could model an example of a flow chart or time line on the board.

Spend some time going over their ideas and suggestions.

ACTIVITY 2

Read the opening of the story titled 'The Visitor' with the students and ask them, in pairs, to think about how the story could develop.

Encourage them to look for any hints/clues that could help them. As an exercise to embed the skills of the previous section, ask students to highlight any examples of interesting vocabulary/imagery.

Here are some examples they might select:

- 'velvet blackness of the night sky'
- 'The relentless rain spat'
- 'zigzagging'
- 'angry rain'
- 'fierce wind bellowing an aggressive symphony'

Ask students to predict what might happen next. Collate ideas/suggestions and discuss how they arrived at these conclusions.

Then encourage students to plan and write the whole story. When they have finished, ask them to reassess their writing. They should come up with two things they are satisfied with and two areas for improvement, which could be their targets for their next piece of writing.

Step 2 | Practise your skills

Explain to students that creating believable characters will help them produce a successful story. Ask them what techniques they think might help in the creation of character.

ACTIVITY 3

Ask students to read the description of a character from *The Hundred Thousand Kingdoms*. They should underline the adjectives and think about what these words suggest about the character's personality.

Here are some aspects they might explore:

- 'Face like the moon, pale and somehow wavering.'
- 'long, long hair'
- 'like black smoke'
- 'unfelt wind'
- 'lurked' sounds sinister and secretive as if he is hiding something about his real character

Point out to the students that it is often more effective to give clues about a character's personality and suggest it rather than stating it explicitly. To exemplify this you could adopt different poses, for example, folded arms, for the students to guess how you are feeling. This could easily be adapted into a whole-class role-play activity.

Unit 13 Communicating imaginatively

ACTIVITY 4

Read the description of Curley's wife from *Of Mice and Men* and ask students, in pairs, to complete the table to show what they have worked out about her character and personality.

Description	What it suggests
'rectangle of sunshine was cut off'	She has an ominous, unsettling presence.
'A girl'	Makes her sound young, impressionable and vulnerable; the indefinite article makes her sound insignificant and unimportant
'looking in'	Suggests she might feel isolated and doesn't feel as if she really belongs or fits in; it could suggest her desire and need to be accepted
'full rouged lips'; 'heavily made up'; 'finger nails were red'	Suggests she wants to stand out from the crowd and be noticed; red is often associated with danger so perhaps she will be a dangerous character; she wants to look glamorous and seems as if she spends a lot of time on her appearance; perhaps she is vain or maybe she is bored and has nothing else to do with her time
'She wore a cotton house dress'	Might suggest that she feels trapped in her role as a woman; perhaps she feels trapped in the 'house'
'red mules, on the insteps of which were little bouquets of red ostrich feathers'	Suggests again that she wants to create a glamorous impression; the reference to the ostrich feathers might suggest her desire to escape and fly away from her current situation, but just as an ostrich is a flightless bird, her escape is also impossible and she feels trapped
'Her voice had a nasal, brittle quality.'	Suggests her voice has a slightly grating and irritating sound and also perhaps she has a weaker and more fragile side to her character

Spend some time going over and collating these responses and suggestions.

ACTIVITY 5

Ask students to read the next description and try to work out how the writer makes us think that Lord Asriel is a dangerous and threatening character. Here are some details they might want to focus on:

- 'a tall man with powerful shoulders' – suggests he is physically a large and intimidating presence
- 'fierce dark face' – suggests a sinister and ominous side to his character; he could be easily angered
- 'eyes that seemed to flash' – suggests a sudden and dangerous temper; not a man to be crossed
- 'glitter with savage laughter' – suggests even his laughter has a sinister, fierce and vicious quality
- 'his movements were… like those of a wild animal' – suggests he is dangerous, unpredictable and vicious; he has the qualities of a hunter or predator
- 'he seemed a wild animal held in a cage too small for it' – suggests he feels entrapped?

Spend some time going over and discussing ideas and suggestions.

To practise describing a character's feeling by using body language, ask students to complete this task in pairs. Here are some points they might think of:

Description of body language	Most likely feelings
Looking down and not making eye contact	Embarrassed/shy/guilty
Eyes wide open and staring	Shock/amazement/surprise/fear
Folding arms and frowning	Bad mood/annoyed/disappointed
Growing redder in the face	Anger/embarrassment/shame
Hands behind head with elbows stretched out	Relaxed/lazy/pleased/complacent/smug
Raising eyebrows and shaking head	Disbelieving/sceptical/disagreement
Shrugging shoulders	Nonchalant/uncaring
Tapping foot or fingers	Nervous/irritated/anxious/bored
Pointing at a person while talking	Aggressive/rude/intimidating
Winking	Joking/flirting/teasing

Spend some time going over the suggestions and collating answers.

Writing Units

Next, ask students to study the pictures and write a physical description of each character to suggest what he/she is like. The teacher could complete a description and model it on the board as an example. They could also think about using similes and metaphors here. Spend some time going over and discussing their ideas.

ACTIVITY 6

Help students develop the idea of suggesting instead of stating by practising describing the movement of a character.

Students can mix and match characteristics and activities from the columns and write a paragraph to practise their skills. Spend time going over these and ask students to try to guess what characteristic and activity are being described.

ACTIVITY 7

Focus students' attention on describing how a character might speak. Ask them to think of ten alternative words to describe how a character might speak instead of using the verb 'said'.

Students should think about what the verb would suggest about how the character is feeling. You could model a couple of examples on the board. Spend some time collating and discussing the suggestions.

ACTIVITY 8

Read the account of a menacing teacher. Ask students to pick out some of the effective words/descriptions. Here are some points students might want to explore:

- 'all forced out of our seat by invisible springs'
- 'two shiny black shoes'
- 'He stood like an army general'
- 'ready to bark'
- 'black malevolent eyes scanned the room threateningly'
- 'he slowly marched'
- 'gleaming white teeth'
- 'His hair was dark silver and closely shaven'
- 'he growled'

Go over and discuss suggestions from the class. Ask students to think about what these details suggest about the character. Then ask students to create a description of an intimidating character of their own.

Share responses with the class.

Step 3 Challenge yourself

ACTIVITY 9

Take students through the section on how to create and suggest a type of setting or atmosphere.

Read the extract from *Bleak House* with the students and ask them to pick out words that create atmosphere.

Answers
- 'Fog'
- 'waterside pollution'
- 'Fog creeping'
- 'wheezing'
- 'cruelly pinching'
- 'shivering boys'
- 'fog all around them'
- 'misty clouds'

Here are some possible answers to the next set of questions:

- Short sentence for emphasis: 'London… Fog everywhere.'
- Repetition for effect: 'Fog up the river… fog down the river'
- Interesting and effective verbs: 'flows'; 'creeping'; 'hovering'; 'drooping'; 'wheezing'; 'peeping'
- A simile: 'as if they were up in a balloon'
- Effective adjectives: 'great'; 'dirty'; 'ancient'; 'shivering'; 'misty'

Spend some time going over the answers and ask students what these details suggest about the place and atmosphere.

ACTIVITY 10

Ask students to study the pictures of a deserted beach in winter and a busy beach in summer.

Encourage them to think of what sort of atmosphere they would create for each one.

Here are a few possibilities:
- Winter – lonely, deserted, silent, cold
- Summer – loud, colourful, lively, vibrant

Then ask students to think of similes and metaphors they could include in each setting.

Students should then write a few paragraphs about each setting. Read responses aloud and discuss word choices with the class.

BE EXAM READY

LEARNING OBJECTIVES

▶ To feel confident about writing a creative response within a set time
▶ To feel confident about how to improve my writing

Take students through the introductory section about how to tackle this part of the exam paper.

Question 1

Ask students to read the dos and don'ts section to ascertain how prepared they feel about this aspect of their assessment.

Answers

Do this in the exam?	✓/✗
Use paragraphs and sentences of various lengths.	✓
Don't bother planning before you start writing.	✗
Use precise adjectives and verbs.	✓
Relax when you finish writing the story and wait for the exam to finish.	✗
Include as many characters as you can.	✗
Choose the first title on the list without reading the whole list of choices.	✗
Use some dialogue to help reveal character.	✓
Check spelling and punctuation.	✓
Have a strong, intriguing opening.	✓

Go over and discuss these answers.

Question 2

In order to practise these skills give students the list of titles in the Student's Book and ask them to choose the title that would best suit them. Then ask them to plan the story in a format that is helpful to them in just 10 minutes (the time suggested in the exam).

Spend time recapping what they need to remember and include and then encourage them to write the story in 35 minutes (the time suggested in the exam).

This then provides an opportunity for peer-/self-assessment. Ask students to write down two things they feel they did well. Go over these points. Ask them to write down two areas where they need to improve. Go over these points and encourage students to use these as their targets for their next creative responses later in this section.

Question 3

Ask students to read the extracts from creative prose responses and to decide whether they are good examples of creative writing or not. Here are some points they might consider:

- Extract A: uses short sentences; questions to suggest reflection; ellipsis to create suspense and tension.
- Extract B: not a successful piece of writing; lacks variety of sentence structure; lacks dramatic opening; contains irrelevant details; lacks ambitious vocabulary.

Spend some time going over and discussing responses.

Next students should compare the sample answers in response to 'A Day at the Seaside'. Here are some points they might make:

Text A

Uses dialogue but it isn't punctuated correctly; errors in spelling; equiptment (equipment), carn't (can't), nowere (nowhere), of (off), aaron (Aaron), wes sat (we sat) beachs's (beaches), fosh (fish); good vocabulary is used; engaging and interesting but points need to be developed.

Targets would be to use paragraphs, to vary sentence structures and to include more description and imagery.

Text B

Engaging; descriptive; ambitious vocabulary and figurative language used.

Spend some time going over and discussing these responses.

Writing Units

Question 4

Ask students to consider the list of story titles in the Student's Book and to choose the question they feel they would best be suited to.

They should write the plan in 10 minutes. Bearing in mind the targets set earlier in the section, students should write the story in 35 minutes.

When they have finished, encourage students to evaluate what they have written. They could annotate their response with the colour coding, such as:

- Blue – interesting and ambitious vocabulary
- Green – new paragraphs and direct speech
- Red – literary techniques such as similes, metaphors, personfication
- Yellow – adjectives and adverbs
- Black – setting
- Pencil – errors in spelling and punctuation

Ask the students to think about how they can improve their writing. For example, if they haven't highlighted much of their work in yellow it tells them that they haven't used many adjectives and adverbs.

This will enable students to see at a glance in what areas they need to improve and develop their skills.

Spend time going over these responses.

Encourage students to decide upon three targets to improve their performance. Go over these.

Extension Activity 1

Choose one of the following titles for your writing:

1. The Wedding
2. Write about a time when you won something.
3. Continue with the following: 'Some days can only get better...'
4. The Time of My Life

Extension Activity 2

Choose one of the following titles for your writing:

1. The Meeting
2. Write about a time when you volunteered to do something.
3. Write a story that begins: 'Just go and ask her,' Sam said. 'There's no harm in asking.'
4. The Letter

Extension Activity 3

Choose one of the following titles for your writing:

1. The Prize
2. Write about an occasion that turned out better than expected.
3. Continue the following: 'The news was terrible. They were actually closing the place down...'
4. Write a story that ends with the following: ' ... I wish I had never, ever thought of buying it.'

Extension Activity 4

Choose one of the following titles for your writing:

1. The Traitor
2. Write about an incident when you were embarrassed by your friends or family.
3. Write about an occasion when you appeared on stage.
4. Write a story that begins: 'He hoped he would have the strength to do what was right.'

Unit 14
Style and register, purpose and audience

LEARNING OBJECTIVES

▶ To use the appropriate register and style for different types of text
▶ To understand why I am writing (purpose) and who will read it (audience)

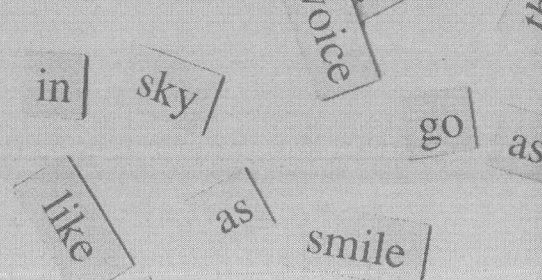

Assessment Objectives

AO5 ■ Communicate clearly, effectively and imaginatively selecting and adapting tone, style and register for different forms, purposes and audiences.
■ Organise information and ideas to support coherence and cohesion of texts using structural and grammatical features.
AO6 ■ Use a range of vocabulary and sentence structure for clarity, purpose and effect with accurate spelling and punctuation.

Ask students to look at the 'How confident are you...' table to assess prior learning and confidence.

Read through the introductory paragraph with students and explain how they will be faced with different texts in school and in the world of work in later life.

Begin by asking students to write a list of all the different text types they can think of and the different types of audiences that may be asked to write for.

Spend time going over the suggestions.

Then, take students through the list of key terms.

Get going

Step 1 Work on your skills

ACTIVITY 1

You could begin by reading aloud the list of questions in the Student's Book and asking the students to decide on the purpose for each one: to inform, to persuade, to entertain or a combination of more than one of these.

This exercise could be worked by using whiteboards or by holding up cards with the purpose written on them. Here are the answers students will probably come up with:

a To inform
b To inform and entertain
c To inform and persuade
d To inform and persuade
e To inform and entertain
f To inform and entertain

Spend some time going over the answers and discussing the reasons for such choices.

ACTIVITY 2

Reading aloud the extract from the speech to the students might be a useful way into this activity. Then, arrange students into pairs and ask them to write a list of possible points they could include to extend the speech.

Spend some time discussing possible ideas and deciding which ones would be more appropriate.

Then ask students to think about what persuasive techniques they would want to include if they wanted to 'sell' themselves and encourage their peers to vote for them.

97

Writing Units

Spend some time discussing and going over their suggestions. They might come up with possibilities such as:

- questions
- exclamations
- ellipses
- repetition for effect
- adjectives
- emotive vocabulary.

Ask students to write their own version of the speech. Students could read out their responses to the class and these could then be peer-assessed with students voting for the most persuasive and convincing speech.

ACTIVITY 3

Explain to students the importance of knowing who the intended audience will be for any piece of writing as this will affect their language, register and style of writing.

Ask students who they think the intended audience would be for the books suggested in the Student's Book.

Here are some suggestions they may think of:

- *The Internet for Dummies* – someone interested in learning about the internet. It is for 'dummies' so probably it would be a beginner who needs to know the basics; any age group
- *A Biography of Lady Gaga* – a music fan/Lady Gaga fan who is interested in finding out details about her life: possibly a teenager/adult below middle age?
- *The Official Club History of Chelsea Football Club* – a Chelsea/football fan or anyone who wants to know all the details about the club
- *Easy Meals in 30 Minutes* – someone who enjoys cooking but perhaps has not yet mastered complicated recipes. An adult or someone who does not have a lot of time to prepare meals because of a busy lifestyle

Spend some time going through the answers and discussing the reasoning behind their decisions.

ACTIVITY 4

Ask students to decide whether they think the article might appeal to a teenage audience.

They may say that the choice of film is appropriate; but the article probably would not appeal because the tone is 'flat' and 'lifeless'; the sentence structure is predictable and not varied; the vocabulary isn't very interesting.

Ask students what techniques they would use to make the article more interesting. They may suggest:

- emotive language
- more adjectives
- puns
- ellipses
- questions
- alliteration, etc.

Ask students, in pairs, to rewrite and improve the opening.

Go through the improved responses and discuss the changes.

ACTIVITY 5

Students should notice that this piece of writing is intended to be a speech. 'Thank you for listening' may be what enables them to identify it as such.

They should suggest that the point of the speech was to inform and persuade the listeners that mobile phones are beneficial – 'I hope that with my points you will say it is a blessing', 'I must say it is a huge blessing on our part.'

The audience is peers/school students:

- 'Do you ever wonder why the teachers hate mobiles?'
- 'Because they can't use them?'
- 'Great isn't it?'
- 'All we need now is for them to make you dinner and do your homework (just kidding, Mrs Smith)'

They should suggest that the register is lively and humorous ('They may have more knowledge and more experience but they can't cheat in pub quizzes by using the internet or send each other amusing pictures').

Spend time going over and discussing answers at each stage.

Read through the Top tips with students and explain the important points.

ACTIVITY 6

You could structure this activity by asking students first what sort of information they might include in this kind of article. Collate the suggestions as a class.

Ask them for some techniques they might want to use to begin with. Collate and go over the suggestions.

You could model the opening paragraph using some of the suggestions.

Then, ask students to write their own response.

When students have finished, this could be used as an opportunity for peer-/self-assessment.

Unit 14 Style and register, purpose and audience

ACTIVITY 7

Share the exam-style question with the class. If necessary, help them to identify the purpose, audience and register for the task.

Before students begin to write their own response, it would be a useful time to recap on the tips about using paragraphs (focused on in Unit 12).

Read through the Top tips about the suitability of language and with the class look at the differences between the two versions in terms of tone and vocabulary.

Ask students to write their own article and spend some time going over responses as a class.

Step 2 Practise your skills

Read through the opening section about how to use a formal and informal register. You could ask students for some examples of slang or text language and explain why they would not be appropriate for any writing task.

ACTIVITY 8

Read the list of tasks and ask students to decide whether the register for the task should be formal or informal. Here are the answers they might come up with:

- application – formal
- friend considering giving up his/her job – informal
- council – formal
- hotel manager – formal
- sister – informal
- friend thinking of becoming a teacher – informal

Go over the answers and discuss how students reached their conclusions.

ACTIVITY 9

Ask students to read the exam-style question (individually or as a class) and to pick out the key pieces of information for the task. Here are the answers students will probably give:

- Purpose – to inform and persuade
- Audience – council members who are intelligent and busy adults
- Register and language – formal/no slang
- Topic – recycling and reducing waste
- Layout – formal letter

Go over the answers and discuss suggestions with class.

Read the Top tips with students and encourage them to use a highlighter pen to help identify the key features of a question in the exam.

ACTIVITY 10

Read the student response to the question in Activity 9. Ask students why they think the response is too informal for the intended audience. Suggested answers might include:

- incorrect layout
- language too informal – 'Dear Council'; 'kids'; 'a stupid and pathetic idea'; 'to dump my rubbish'; 'How would you like it?'
- tone is quite aggressive and rude – 'you lot at the council'; 'What do you think were paying you to do?'; 'How dare you say you are going to fine me.'

Then ask students to think of more appropriate examples for these phrases.

Ask students to think of three pieces of advice they would give to improve the answer. Here are some ideas they might respond with:

- Use the correct layout for a formal letter.
- Use the correct greeting of 'Dear Sir or Madam'.
- Use the correct formal ending of 'Yours faithfully' rather than 'Thank you for listening to me' – it is a letter not a speech.
- Technical accuracy in spelling needs to be improved – rubish (rubbish); were (we're); dont (don't); rediculous (ridiculous).

Students should then rewrite the letter.

Ask students, in pairs, to make a list of ideas that could make the rest of the letter more detailed and interesting. Discuss possible answers and suggestions.

Ask students to sequence their ideas in the best possible order to produce a fluent and coherent letter. Discuss possible answers and suggestions.

Ask students to think of connectives they could use to link ideas and paragraphs. Go over and discuss possible suggestions.

Read the Top tips with the students and explain/model how to set out a formal letter correctly.

Students should then rewrite the letter.

When students have completed the letter, ask them to find and label the key layout features on their own letter, as in the Student's Book example. Ask them to reflect on the vocabulary and sentence structures they have used. Ask them to make any improvements.

Writing Units

ACTIVITY 11

Begin by recapping the differences between formal and informal letters.

Ask students:
- whether they think the register is appropriate for the audience (Yes)
- whether the tone is appropriate (Yes – entertaining and friendly)
- if there is anything that could be done to improve the letter (Write more? Develop the points in more detail?)

Ask students to think of any ideas that could extend each paragraph by three/four sentences each. Discuss ideas and suggestions with the class.

Go through the Top tips with students and help them to complete the table so they can see the differences at a glance between the two types of letters.

Answers

Informal letters	Formal letters
Address of writer in the top right-hand corner	Address of writer in top right-hand corner
Date written underneath in full (can be abbreviated)	Date written underneath in full (no abbreviation)
Address of recipient not used	Address of recipient underneath date on left
Begin: Dear Kath	Formal letters begin with 'Dear Sir or Madam' or with the title and surname of the reader 'Dear Mr Smith'
Informal ending: Best wishes	'Yours faithfully' (if the greeting is Dear Sir or Madam) or 'Yours sincerely (if the greeting is Mr…)

Go through and discuss the answers with the class.

ACTIVITY 12

Read the exam-style question with the class. Go over the:
- purpose (to inform and persuade)
- audience (busy headteacher/school principal)
- register (formal)
- special features (emotive vocabulary, questions, exclamations, ellipses)
- layout (formal letter).

Ask students to write the letter.

This could be a useful opportunity for self-assessment. Work through the checklist in the Student's Book.

Step 3 | Challenge yourself

ACTIVITY 13

Ask students to decide whether the adjectives in this list would create a positive or negative impression. Here are the answers students should come up with:

- mesmerising (positive)
- sophisticated (positive)
- boring (negative)
- stimulating (positive)
- moving (positive)
- exhilarating (positive)
- unconvincing (negative)
- flat (negative)
- unoriginal (negative)
- thrilling (positive)
- disappointing (negative)
- inspiring (positive
- monotonous (negative)
- dull (negative)
- mundane (negative)
- awesome (negative)
- shocking (positive)

Spend some time going over and discussing suggestions with the class.

Ask students to think of six adjectives they could use in their own review writing. Then they should decide whether these adjectives create a positive or negative impression. Spend time going over and discussing suggestions with the class.

Ask students to write a sentence for each adjective to practise how to use them. Go over these sentences and discuss ideas.

ACTIVITY 14

Read the album review with the class and ask them whether they think it would appeal to a teenage audience. They should think the text has a lively tone and the style is interesting and entertaining – so, yes.

Unit 14 Style and register, purpose and audience

Ask students to identify the list of special features in the review. Here are some possible areas the students might explore:

- paragraphs and ideas that are organised clearly
- a lively and entertaining opening sentence ('It's not often you come across a new album that you can genuinely describe as phenomenal,...')
- details of the songs ('The live version of "While We're Young" rips off the intro to...'; 'The chorus of "Kiss You" is hard to get out of your brain'; '"Rock Me", however, is pretty excruciating'; '"Do You Remember the Summer of '09?" they ask')
- strengths of the album ('a new album that you can genuinely describe as phenomenal'; 'isn't bad as albums by boy bands go')
- weaknesses of the album ('Elsewhere the material is of variable quality'; '"Rock Me", however, is pretty excruciating')
- a final paragraph to sum up the writer's opinion and recommendation ('It isn't bad as albums by boy bands go nor, though, is there anything to appeal to anyone except their legions of female fans.')

Spend some time going over and discussing answers.

ACTIVITY 15

Ask students to read the opening of the review and answer the question.

They should think the paragraph is lively and entertaining because it has a list of words to engage the reader and uses rhetorical question to involve the reader.

Then, ask students to look at the *X Factor* review and answer the question.

Here, they should think that the short sentences would appeal and a lively tone is created by words like 'plonked'.

Ask students to write their own review of a TV programme using the techniques they have been studying.

After the self-assessment, the two things each student should improve on can become the targets for their next piece of writing.

Improve your skills

LEARNING OBJECTIVES

▶ To develop a secure approach to writing in different formats
▶ To plan my points effectively

Step 1 Work on your skills

ACTIVITY 1

Ask students to think about the sort of topics they think they might have to write a report about in relation to school and the wider community. They might offer some of these suggestions:

- School – to head/governors about school facilities/sports equipment/problem of bullying/reducing waste/recycling/being more environmentally aware/how to spend a cash donation to the school
- Wider community – facilities for young people

Spend some time going over and collating these suggestions.

Then, recap on topic sentences (covered in Unit 12). Ask students to select one school-related topic and one wider community topic from their suggestions. Students can swap their ideas with a partner and compare and discuss ideas and suggestions.

Ask students, in pairs, to organise these ideas into a clear and coherent order using connectives. Model writing a topic sentence to introduce each paragraph and then ask students to do the same. Spend some time going over and discussing suggested topic sentences around the class.

101

Writing Units

ACTIVITY 2

Ask students to read the list of statements about report writing and decide whether each statement is true or false.

Answers

Report writing	True or false
Reports should be written in formal English.	True
A report should be clearly organised into clear and logical paragraphs.	True
The purpose of a report is to entertain the reader.	False
You need to end a report with 'Yours sincerely' and a signature.	False
A report should have a clear title saying who the intended audience is and the purpose.	True
Your report needs to be 300–400 words in length.	False
A report should be written in columns like a newspaper.	False
Subheadings should be used to make the different sections clear.	True
A report should have pictures to grab the attention of the reader and illustrate what you are talking about.	False

Ask students, in pairs, to design a list or a helpsheet/revision sheet to explain to their peers the special features of report writing based on everything they have learnt so far. Spend some time going over this activity and comparing ideas.

ACTIVITY 3

Read through the exam-style question with the class. Take students through the steps to help them plan and structure their responses in the exam. Encourage students to underline/highlight the key words in the question.

ACTIVITY 4

Ask students to jot down a possible heading for the report. Go over suggestions and discuss ideas/word choices here. Then ask students to think of four or five subheadings they could use to organise and divide their ideas. Go over suggestions and collate ideas around the class.

Now ask students to come up with a topic sentence to begin the first paragraph under each subheading. Spend some time going over and discussing these suggestions.

Students should decide that response A is the more appropriate. Ask students to explain their answer:

- More detail
- Lists the reader and the writer
- States the purpose
- Uses headings
- Includes an introduction

Three things they might suggest to improve in Response B:

- The name and position of the reader
- The name and position of the writer
- The purpose of the report
- An introduction
- More details
- A more polite and less blunt tone

This provides an opportunity for peer-/self-assessment. Ask students to swap their work with a peer and to consider the checklist of questions in the Student's Book in relation to the work in front of them.

Ask the peer marker to suggest two areas for improvement before returning the work to its 'owner'. Spend some time discussing possible areas for improvement with the students.

Step 2 Practise your skills

Read through the introduction on article writing and draw the students' attention to the important points. Explain the key terms of irony and sarcasm to the students and ask them to give/make some examples to check their understanding.

ACTIVITY 5

Ask students to read the review 'Whatever Happened to Rock and Roll?'

It is clearly effective and students should notice that this is largely because of the use of adjectives and verbs. Ask students to pick out some effective words and to be prepared to explain how effective they are. Here are some areas they might want to explore:

- 'the smoky, leathery voice of an old bluesman' (suggests the rasping, unusual quality of his voice which almost belongs to a different era)
- 'one of the most distinctive vocalists' (suggests an easily recognisable voice – no one else can sing like him)

Unit 14 Style and register, purpose and audience

- 'reeling, glittering guitar solos' (suggest his music and skill will knock you off your feet and blow you away; suggests he is special and his skill and talent make him stand out from other musicians)
- 'like gold nuggets in the Dust Bowl' (suggests their songs and skills are precious and rare and stand out from the mediocrity around them)
- 'struts and pouts' (suggests he has stage presence and charisma and is a natural showman/entertainer/performer)

Spend some time going over and discussing answers and suggestions.

Ask students to think of their favourite band/singer and to list any special qualities about their songs or the way they perform. Then ask them to think of some verbs and adjectives to describe their songs/movements/stage presence/effect on audience. Encourage them to use techniques such as alliteration, similes and metaphors here. Spend some time discussing ideas and suggestions.

When students have finished writing their paragraphs, spend some time reading answers aloud and discussing word choices. Students could build up a word bank to include suggestions from the whole class.

ACTIVITY 6

Ask students to look at the less complimentary article about Simon Cowell. Remind students that sarcasm is often used when creating a negative tone in an article and ask them to identify the sarcastic words/phrases in this extract.

They might suggest the following:
- 'The human version of Marmite!'
- 'The smug, super rich fan of seriously untrendy high-waisted trousers'

Ask students to find other techniques that are used successfully in the article. Here are some points they might explore:

- Direct appeal – 'You either love him or hate him' (Involves the readers directly and encourages them to question their own feelings.)
- Exclamations – 'The human version of Marmite!'; 'just by opening his mouth!' (Suggests shock, surprise and the strength of feeling by the writer.)
- Emotive language – 'smug, super rich'; 'smarmy, self-satisfied grin' (Creates a negative impression and makes him sound unpleasant, arrogant and complacent.)

Ask students to think of other techniques that add to the effectiveness of the article. They might think about:
- the use of humour ('television's very own Mr Nasty')
- alliteration ('smug, super rich'; 'smarmy, self-satisfied').

Go over suggestions and comments about word choices.

Ask students to continue the article by writing another two or three paragraphs using some of the effective techniques they have been learning about.

Spend some time reading and sharing examples of good practice around the class.

ACTIVITY 7

Read through the exam-style question with the class and encourage students to focus on the useful points in the Top tips box. Take students through the points on how to plan and structure their responses and model each section on the board as you work through the structure.

Ask students to write their article. When they have finished it provides an opportunity for peer-/self-assessment. Using the checklist in the Student's Book, ask students or peers to evaluate their work objectively and make any improvements they think are needed. Spend some time going over feedback comments.

Ask students to give themselves two targets/areas for development based on this activity. Make sure that each student is able to tell you what his/her targets are.

Step 3 Challenge yourself

ACTIVITY 8

Students should identify that the speech (by Old Major) is effective.

Then, ask students to identify the persuasive techniques and explain why they are effective.

Here are some areas they might explore:
- A persuasive address – 'comrades' (suggests speaker identifies with audience and creates sense of unity because they want the same thing)

103

Writing Units

- Questions/rhetorical questions – 'what is the nature of this life of ours?'; 'is this simply part of the order of nature?'; 'Is it because this land of ours is so poor…?' (directly involves the audience and encourages them to question themselves and their own actions)
- Use of first person plural – 'we'; 'our lives' (creates a sense of unity and togetherness)
- Emotive language – 'just so much food'; 'forced to work to the last atom of our strength' (stirs emotions in the audience)
- Negative language – 'slaughtered'; 'hideous cruelty'; 'misery and slavery' (stresses the horror of the situation and their desperate need to improve it)
- Repetition – 'No animal in England' (to emphasise the unfairness of their situation and their right to a better life)
- Exclamations – 'a thousand times no!' (suggests the speaker's strength of feeling and outrage)

Spend some time going over, collating and discussing answers.

Ask students, in pairs and using the persuasive techniques they have been practising, to write a short persuasive speech on the topics in the list. Read the responses in class and ask students to decide which speech is the most persuasive, giving reasons in support of their decision.

ACTIVITY 9

Students should read through the exam-style question and work out whether they think the student response is successful in persuading an audience. Ask them why/why not.

Focus students' attention on ways to improve the response by asking for specific advice under the suggested headings. Here are some points they might want to explore:

- Format – could have an introduction which involves audience such as 'Hello, Year 11…'.
- Register – is formal and generally appropriate but needs to be more persuasive.
- Vocabulary – is not ambitious and needs more variety; 'support' is used four times; vocabulary needs to be more emotive to make the audience feel guilty if they do not take action.
- Sentence structure – it does not have a range of simple, compound, complex and minor sentences.
- Technical accuracy – only a couple of minor issues.

Spend some time going over and discussing ideas and suggestions.

Now ask students to improve and continue with the response.

When they have finished, encourage students to compare both versions.

BE EXAM READY

LEARNING OBJECTIVES

▶ To feel confident about using an appropriate register, tone and style for an intended audience

▶ To feel confident about evaluating my work to improve my performance

Read through the introduction about the exam requirements for Section B of Component 2 with students. Make sure they realise that the requirements and marks available are different from the writing task in Component 1.

Question 1

Read through the list of exam-style questions and ask students to write a plan for each question. Time students (or have students time themselves) as they do this and only allow 5 minutes per plan, which is the suggested time they will have in the exam.

Time students to write their response in 25 minutes as suggested in the exam. Remind students that they need to write 300–400 words.

Question 2

This is an opportunity for self-assessment as students evaluate their responses. Ask the question, 'Are you satisfied with what you have written?'

Ask students to read their work carefully and write down two things they feel they have done well. Spend some time discussing these points.

Then ask students to write down two things they need to improve upon. Spend some time discussing these points. Students should use these points as targets for their next piece of writing.

Now give students the assessment/marking criteria and encourage them to work out which band their response would be in.

Question 3

Ask students to choose another one of the Question 1 tasks and write a response in 25 minutes focusing on the targets created by the previous activity. When they have finished, ask students to use the assessment/marking criteria to place their work in the correct band. Ask them what they think they need to do to move up to the next band?

Extension Activity 1

The following is an extract from a letter which appeared in a national newspaper:

> Have we gone mad? We are paying pop stars, sportsmen and women and actors and actresses more in a week than most people earn in a year. When people are homeless or living in poverty, the money paid to these so-called 'stars' is obscene and totally unjustified.

You may agree or disagree with this point of view.

Write a letter to the newspaper giving your views on this issue.

Extension Activity 2

The governors who are responsible for running your school or college are interested in the views of students.

They have asked you to write a report, pointing out what you see as the strengths and weaknesses of your school or college.

You might like to consider some of the following headings for your report, but feel free to choose your own:

- Facilities and equipment
- Buildings
- Range of subjects
- Out-of-school activities

105

Writing Units

Extension Activity 3

Write a lively article for a newspaper or magazine on the subject of the eating habits of the British.

You may use your own ideas but you may also consider one or more of the following:

- 'Typical' British food/non-British food
- Healthy eating/junk food
- Vegetarianism
- Eating in/eating out

Extension Activity 4

Some of the large cities in Britain are proposing a congestion charge on drivers to encourage people to use public transport. This would mean drivers would have to pay every time they went into the city centre.

Write a speech for your peers giving your views on this proposal.

Unit 15
Transactional and persuasive writing

LEARNING OBJECTIVES

▶ To understand the features of transactional and persuasive writing
▶ To write clearly and persuasively

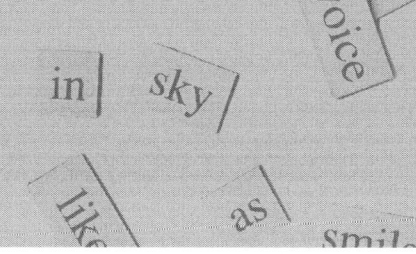

Assessment Objectives

AO5 ■ Communicate clearly, effectively and imaginatively selecting and adapting tone, style and register for different forms, purposes and audiences.
■ Organise information and ideas to support coherence and cohesion of texts using structural and grammatical features.
AO6 ■ Use a range of vocabulary and sentence structure for clarity, purpose and effect with accurate spelling and punctuation.

Explain to students that some texts provide information while some will have an element of persuasion. Make them aware that some texts may do both of these things.

Starter activity

Using whiteboards or pieces of card, ask students to indicate whether the purpose of the following tasks is to inform, persuade or entertain.

- Report about school improvements (inform)
- Review of a pop concert (inform and entertain)
- Job application (inform and persuade)
- Magazine article about a favourite book (inform and entertain)
- Speech about benefits of mobile phones (inform and persuade)
- Letter to friend in hospital (inform and entertain)
- Report about the problem of bullying (inform)

Get going

Step 1 | Work on your skills

To practise this skill of making an impression on your intended audience, ask students to make up a shocking fact or statistic to introduce these topics:

- School uniform
- Exercise
- Smoking
- Social media

Spend some time going over possible answers and suggestions.

Now explain bold and challenging statements to the students.

Ask students to make up bold and challenging statements about the following topics:

- Bullying
- Homework
- Our carbon footprint

Spend some time going over possible answers and suggestions.

107

Writing Units

ACTIVITY 1

Read the exam-style question and ask students what the purpose is of this task. (To inform and persuade)

Students should write three different sentence openings to grab the audience's attention, using each of the techniques (surprising fact or statistic; rhetorical question; bold or challenging statement).

Spend time going over possible answers, suggestions and appropriate alternatives.

Students should decide on their best opening sentence and write the following two or three paragraphs in the speech.

Spend some time asking students to read their work aloud. This could be an opportunity for peer-assessment, with students offering suggestions and alternatives. Students could identify two good features about the response and one area for development/improvement.

Run through the Top tips with the class.

ACTIVITY 2

Students should rewrite these opening sentences to create greater impact on the audience.

Spend some time going over the answers and discussing alternatives with the class. This would also be a useful exercise/opportunity to encourage students to think about the effect of emotive language.

Students should choose their best rewritten sentence and continue to write the next three or four paragraphs in response to the task. They should be encouraged to plan and organise their material, sequencing ideas coherently. This would be a useful opportunity to recap on connectives.

Spend some time going over the answers they have produced. Discuss ideas and the effect of word choices.

There could be a further opportunity for peer-assessment here.

ACTIVITY 3

Using one of these techniques, students should write a final paragraph/conclusion for the response they are working on.

Spend some time discussing various responses with the class.

ACTIVITY 4

This activity focuses on persuasive devices and how effective they can be.

Read the extract from the speech about mobile phones with the class.

In pairs, students should highlight/identify the following techniques.

- Rhetorical questions – 'How many parents would panic if they thought deadly and invisible microwaves were passing through children's brains several times a day?'; 'Aren't parents concerned that their children are slowly frying their brains?'.
  The rhetorical questions are effective because they make the reader/audience question their own behaviour/attitudes. Also they make the reader/audience feel guilt, shock, fear.

- Exclamations – 'in fact they may be even more dangerous!'; 'children under the age of 12 have their own mobiles and use them more than an hour a day!'
  The exclamations are effective because they suggest shock, surprise, outrage.

- Ellipses – 'hand held devices are no safer… in fact they may be even more dangerous!'
  The ellipsis is effective because it creates suspense and tension.

- Emotive adjectives – 'deadly and invisible microwaves' (sounds sinister, threatening and dangerous); 'serious risk' (makes it sound important and frightening); 'even more dangerous' (sounds dramatic and alarming)

- Statistics – '85% of children under the age of 12' (sounds reliable and knowledgeable so we trust the research)

- Expert opinions – 'Medical experts from Oxford University' (top experts are respected and so add weight and authority to the speech; 'survey… by BBC's "Watchdog"' (we trust this authority)

To practise and consolidate these skills, students should write a speech to be delivered to their English teacher persuading him/her not to give any homework.

Encourage students to think about audience, purpose and register.

Students should organise points into the best possible order and think about connectives as well.

When students have finished writing the speech, this can be used as an opportunity for peer-/self-assessment.

Students can be encouraged to highlight examples of persuasive techniques they have learnt and used.

Spend some time listening to answers.

Step 2 Practise your skills

Explain to the class that sometimes persuasive techniques need to be included in letters to make an argument sound convincing and change the viewpoint or opinion of the reader.

ACTIVITY 5

Read out the question and ask students to think about the audience, purpose and register for the task.

Share sample responses with the class and, in pairs, students can answer the questions.

Answers to the student questions:
- The format should be a formal letter because the question asks you to 'write a letter to your local newspaper'.
- The letter has not been set out correctly. For example, addresses have not been used; there is no date; madame should be madam; Yours sincerely should be Yours faithfully.
- The tone of the letter should be more formal.
- The ideas and opinions in the middle paragraphs need to be developed; ideas have only been listed and not exemplified; bullet points should not be used as the criteria for assessing sentence structure.
- The final paragraph asks for action to be taken but the expression is clumsy.
- Technical errors are as follows; madame (madam); opposal (opposition); john smith (John Smith); enfisise (emphasise); dogust (disgust); uneeded (unneeded); eldery (elderly); difficultys (difficulties); conjestion (congestion); peple (people); whicj (which); devasting (devastating); unessacarilly (unnecessarily).

Then, ask students to choose one paragraph from their letter to rewrite. Encourage them to add more detail and more persuasive techniques. They could be told to include one rhetorical question, one exclamation, five examples of emotive language, one ellipsis, etc.

Select a paragraph from a student at random and model improvements on the whiteboard.

Spend some time reading and going over answers around the class.

ACTIVITY 6

This letter is clearly more successful and technically accurate than the previous response.

Students might come up with some of the following reasons why this answer would score more highly:

- It is longer and the ideas are more developed.
- Technically the writing is more accurate.
- Emotive and ambitious vocabulary has been used.
- The sentence structure is varied.
- The argument is convincing.

Persuasive techniques:
- Emotive vocabulary – 'vibrancy', 'amazingly talented', 'excellent', 'good opportunity', 'wonderful'
- Rhetorical questions – 'And for the locals?'; 'Why not be proud of them?'; 'Surely, our usual symphony of roadworks, traffic noise and groups of people who have just exited the pubs is far worse?'; 'what's not to like?'
- Exclamations – 'What a ridiculous idea!'; An outdoor music festival would attract people who love music, not hooligans!'
- Sophisticated vocabulary – 'prodigious'; 'vibrancy'; 'potential'; 'symphony of roadworks'; 'undesirable persons'; 'vast array'

ACTIVITY 7

Ask students, in pairs, to write down a list of benefits and facilities for each of the choices suggested in the question.

Spend some time collating and discussing answers.

Ask students to decide on the purpose (to persuade), the audience (well-educated and knowledgeable adults), layout (formal letter) and register (formal language and tone; no slang).

Encourage students to sequence their ideas, maybe as a flow chart or similar, to present them in the most effective order.

Spend time going over and discussing and sharing their ideas.

Students could be timed to complete the writing of this task in 30 minutes as they will have 1 hour to complete two writing tasks in the exam.

Write a list of persuasive features on the whiteboard and encourage students/peers to highlight and label these features in their own writing/the writing of a partner.

Ask students to think about what could be added to make their writing more persuasive and interesting.

Ask students, using a different coloured pen, to underline any connectives they can find in the writing; if there are no connectives, encourage them to add some.

Writing Units

Ask students to find examples of different types of sentences in their letter. This could be a useful opportunity to revise simple, compound, complex and minor sentences.

Encourage students, in pairs, to think about improving their vocabulary by looking for possible alternatives in a thesaurus.

Spend some time going over and discussing improvements with students.

With these improvements in mind, encourage students to rewrite two or three paragraphs of their letter. Ask them to compare their first and second attempts to see the differences!

Step 3 Challenge yourself

ACTIVITY 8

This task does not need to include persuasive techniques because it is a report.

Ask students to think of three points they could make under each subheading.

ACTIVITY 9

Now read through the exemplar response to the question in Activity 8 with the students.

Inappropriate and informal style:
- 'You wouldn't like standing out in the wind and rain all through lunch times, would you?'
- 'Well,…'
- 'Please, please can you try to give us a common room?'

Encourage students to rewrite these sentences.

They might come up with these suggestions as to how the format could be improved:

- Introduction
- Conclusion
- Who the report is for
- Who the report is from
- Subheadings
- More points

ACTIVITY 10

Read the second response to the same question and the Top tips.

Ask students to find examples of connectives and appropriate vocabulary in the response.

- Connectives – 'Firstly'; 'Secondly'
- Appropriate vocabulary – 'congregate'; 'refuge'; 'controlled environment'

Students should now complete this second response using the ideas they thought of at the start of the section. They should aim to write 300–400 words.

When they have finished this task, ask them to find examples of where they have used a polite and serious tone; a range of different sentence styles (simple/compound/complex/minor); a conclusion.

Spend some time discussing answers in a feedback session.

Ask students to spend some time completing the '… do you think your confidence has increased?' table to assess whether their confidence has increased and whether progress has been made.

Improve your skills

LEARNING OBJECTIVES

▶ To have a secure understanding of how to appeal to an audience
▶ To practise using techniques to improve transactional and persuasive writing

Read through the initial section about review writing with students.

Step 1 Work on your skills

ACTIVITY 1

Ask students to answer the questions after they have read the review and spend some time as a class going over the answers.

Here are some ideas they might come up with:

- The writer's opinion about the film – not totally convinced; 'The jury is still out'; 'Something of a mixed bag then, with several question marks left hanging'
- Positive words – 'back on track'; 'less whimsical waffle'; 'yomping pace'; 'endless array'; 'spectacular sights'; 'eager to dazzle, ready to please'; 'fantastical characters'; 'high tech action sequences'; 'handsomely mounted set pieces'; 'a definite improvement'

- Negative words – 'dawdling disappointment'; 'strung out'; 'a lot of bagginess'; 'the air of a supercharged computer game'
- The review is definitely entertaining: the alliteration of 'dawdling disappointment', 'spectacular sights'; interesting vocabulary and example of onomatopoeia in 'comparatively yomping pace'; 'endless array' – sounds emotive as if the list of possibilities will go on and on. (Hopefully students will notice the use of adjectives in the review.)
- The review includes information about the plot – 'head through the forest of Mirkwood'; 'then to the lost kingdom of Erebor'; 'en route characters ranging from Legolas to the gigantic dragon, Smaug'.
- The review uses different types of sentences: some start with prepositions, 'After the…'; 'With less whimsical waffle…'
- There are many compound and complex sentences.

Ask students to find any interesting words or techniques that they could adopt to improve their own writing. They should be thinking about the use of adjectives, adverbs, alliteration, exclamations, etc.

Spend some time discussing their findings.

ACTIVITY 2

Read the exam-style question with the students and discuss the purpose, audience, register and format for the task.

Ask students to then write the review in 300–400 words.

When students have completed the review, this provides a useful opportunity for peer-/self-assessment.
- Ask students to highlight the words that they think would appeal to teenage readers.
- Ask students to underline all the adjectives they have used. Do they need to include more?
- Encourage students to include more ambitious vocabulary by using a thesaurus.
- Ask students to identify the different types of sentences they have used.

Spend some time going over suggestions, alternatives and answers.

Encourage students to improve and rewrite one paragraph from their own review using skills from the previous activity.

Spend some time going over answers and consolidating skills.

ACTIVITY 3

Here are some answers they might suggest:
- Two ways in which the opening catches the attention of the reader – the use of a rhetorical question 'Dropping England's best player over the five years, for whom? Andy Carroll?'; the use of emotive vocabulary 'downright laughable'.
- Sarcasm is found in the mocking tone of 'for whom? Andy Carroll?'
- There are examples of different types of sentences: minor sentences – 'Until now.'; 'Andy Carroll?': -ing sentences – 'Dropping Rooney is, amazingly, the smart move.': complex sentences – 'For years, the idea of England dropping Wayne Rooney has rarely been discussed – in fact it was downright laughable.'

ACTIVITY 4

Read the exam-style question with the students and ask them to underline the key words in the question. (lively; article; teenagers)

Ask students to decide on the purpose, audience, register and format for the task. (inform and entertain; teenagers; informal; article with a catchy heading)

Work through the model of a possible structure for the article with the students, pausing frequently to collate and go over answers/suggestions.

Ask students to write the article.

Reading through the work provides an opportunity for peer-/self-assessment.

Step 2 | Practise your skills

Read through the section about writing a 'rough guide' with students and draw attention to the main points.

ACTIVITY 5

Read through the exam-style question and ask students to identify the purpose, audience, register and format for the task (to inform and entertain; any age group; clear and informal; similar to an article).

Writing Units

ACTIVITY 6

Read the student response to the task and encourage students to pick out any vocabulary that lacks sophistication ('nice'; 'nice and clean'; 'white'; 'clear blue'; 'pleasant').

Ask students to use a thesaurus to improve the word choices.

Ask students to identify any sentences they think could be improved ('Last summer I visited a nice coast in Spain called Costa Del Sol.'; 'In the camp there was a choice of caravan camping, tents and chalets.'; 'You think of a shop and it was there.').

Spend some time discussing possible alternatives.

ACTIVITY 7

Read the sample response and ask the students to identify and correct the technical errors:

- europes – Europe's
- muesium – museum
- eurpoean – European
- have – has
- Oolympic – Olympic
- zii – zoo
- europes – Europe's
- albeano – albino
- nightime – night time
- its – it is
- loverly – lovely

New paragraphs could begin as follows:

- Barcelona also has…
- There is also a wonderful…
- Not too far from there…
- If that is not enough…
- If it's just the quiet…

Ask students to think of three ways in which this response could be made more interesting and entertaining, perhaps in groups. Students might suggest some of the following:

- more descriptive adjectives
- questions
- sentence variety
- exclamations
- ellipses

Now ask students to rewrite this response.

ACTIVITY 8

Ask students to read the student response and pick out some words that would appeal to the reader. Students might offer the following suggestions:

- 'beautifully cobbled Bold Street'
- 'alternative and "one-off" boutiques'
- 'cash to flash'
- 'sophisticated cuisine and alfresco dining'

Spend some time going over answers.

Ask students to write their own entry about a place they know well. Encourage them to organise their ideas and collate suggestions.

Step 3 Challenge yourself

ACTIVITY 9

Ask students to read the jumbled paragraphs from a speech about fireworks. This could be done as a sorting exercise for students to rearrange into the correct order.

Paragraph 1	Bonfire Night is meant to…
Paragraph 2	Little Emma Jenkins…
Paragraph 3	Of course, not only humans are affected…
Paragraph 4	The time has come to stop…
Paragraph 5	No! Now is the time…

Ask students to make a list of more ideas they could include for this speech.

Spend some time going over suggestions.

Students should write the speech using the persuasive techniques they have learnt.

This provides an opportunity for peer-/self-assessment.

Ask students to underline any examples of ambitious or sophisticated vocabulary and different types of sentences.

Spend some time going over their responses.

Ask students to write down three things they are pleased with in their response and two areas in which they need to improve.

Spend time discussing these points with students.

112

ACTIVITY 10

Read the extract from the speech about the need to improve facilities in the school/college canteen with the students.

Persuasive techniques might include:

- rhetorical question –'Have you ever attempted to eat your lunch in the school's canteen…?' – encourages direct involvement by asking reader to question own behaviour and attitudes
- emotive vocabulary – 'brave enough'; 'risk'; 'appallingly noisy'; 'unappealing'; 'precious lunch hour'; 'endless queue'
- use of figures/statistics – '1600 hungry students'.

Students should aim to write the next three paragraphs for this task.

BE EXAM READY

LEARNING OBJECTIVES

▶ To feel confident about writing clearly and persuasively in the exam
▶ To feel confident about improving my performance

Question 1

Read the question and ask students to identify the important words in the question (talk; group of older people; persuade).

Check these answers with students.

Students should write a plan for this task in 5 minutes.

Question 2

Ask students to read the sample response and give three pieces of advice on how it could be improved.

Go over these suggestions. Students might suggest the following areas for improvement:

- Tone
- Points need to be developed and expanded upon
- More emotive language
- More persuasive techniques

Question 3

Read the next response with the students and compare the answers.

Time students as they write their own response of 300–400 words in 25 minutes.

Question 4

Ask students to study the exam-style question and then the sample answer.

They might consider the following points the student does well:

- Generally sensible ideas
- Some good vocabulary – 'probability', 'under the influence of alcohol or other substances'

They might come up with the following points for how to improve the response:

- The ideas are not always fully developed.
- The writing is not always technically accurate.
- The vocabulary could be more emotive.
- The ending is a bit rushed.

Question 5

Students should spend 5 minutes writing a plan for each of the five titles for the writing tasks.

Spend some time with the class going over each task.

Students should choose one of the tasks from the list in the previous activity. Time students and allow them 25 minutes to write their answer.

Ask students to assess their work – either individually or in pairs.

Spend some time going round all the students to ascertain their individual targets and areas for improvement.

Question 6

As a homework task students should choose one of the other tasks and complete the writing in 25 minutes.

Extension Activity

For extra practice students could be encouraged to work through these writing tasks.

They should spend 5 minutes planning their answer and 25 minutes writing 300–400 words as a response.

1. During the last year you will have been through the process of deciding what to do after your GCSEs. You may have decided to stay at school, to go to a local college or to look for training or a job.
Write a lively article for your school magazine, which you think would be helpful to next year's leavers when they are faced with the same decisions. You could use the headline 'Is there life after 16?' or you could provide your own.

2. 'TV talent shows (such as *X Factor*) are hugely popular. Some people think they are great because they give unknown people with talent a chance to become famous. Other people think they are put on so that the TV audience watching can laugh at contestants making fools of themselves.'
Write a letter to a newspaper giving your views on TV talent shows.